SURVIVING GOD!

Overcoming the Challenges . . .
in all of our lives!

A book by Ken Guthrie

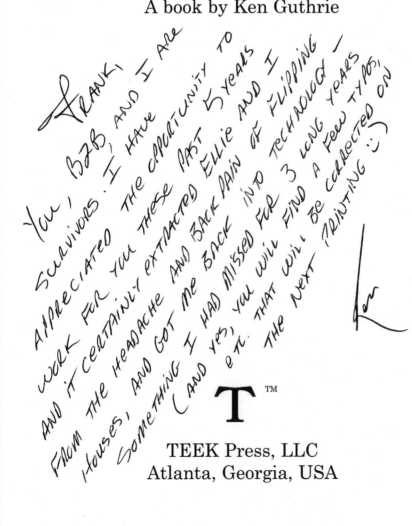

Frank,

You, B2B, and I are survivors! I have appreciated the opportunity to work for you these past 5 years and it certainly extracted Ellie and I from the headache and back pain of flipping houses, and got me back into technology! Something I had missed for 3 long years (and yes, you will find a few typos, etc. that will be corrected on the next printing :)

T™

TEEK Press, LLC
Atlanta, Georgia, USA

Please go to the www.SurvivingGod.com website to
see discounts available for single orders of
10(ten) or more copies of this book.

A recorded version of the book read by the author is
scheduled for release by mid-year 2011.

For my wife Ellie, and sons, Eric and Ty,
for their perseverance, patience, and ability to endure
all of my diverse interests, verboseness, and
badly told jokes over the many years.

Surviving God!

Copyright 2011

ISBN 978-0-9846041-0-4

TEEK Press, LLC
Atlanta Georgia, USA (www.teekpress.com)
Printed in China

Cover photograph, *"Clouds Breaking Blue"* and cover design by the author.

Table of Contents

SURVIVING GOD !

Overcoming the Challenges . . .
in all of our lives!

Introduction:

Mankind has always been challenged by God. Each waking moment, we face as both individuals and as a brotherhood, hurdles that must be overcome to survive. And by survival, I mean not only life, but spirit as well. Within each of us there is an ability to grow and prosper, but only we can choose how we use that gift to meet God's challenges and more importantly, survive them.

Now you might ask is the word "survive" appropriate. We think of survive in terms of living . . . often repeated in phrases as *"survival* of the fittest", or associated with *survivors* from some kind of battle or accident. Well, if that *is* the way you think of the word "survive", then your thoughts are right on track. Why? Because, in one way or another, you and I are survivors, just as Abraham, or Jesus, or the Disciples were survivors, and in each and every case where God challenged them, through their survival they became stronger.

Do we have to sacrifice our children, spouses, or friends as in time of war to be stronger? For some the answer is yes.

I

Do we have to lose all that we hold dear in life, our success, our confidence, or our fortunes to become stronger in God's universe? Possibly so.

Do we have to personally endure physical pain or mental anguish and in that way grow because we survived? Again, the answer can be "yes".

And finally, is it just a matter of living one day at a time and surviving until the next? Yes . . . it *is* living one day at a time and surviving to the next day, and then the next, and the next again.

Each morning when we wake, we run the risk of being hit in the face with what may seem an insurmountable challenge that God has given us. It may not come today, or tomorrow, or even this year, but it *will* come!

Sometimes it is not so much the height or breadth of God's challenge, but more importantly, how we deal with it, and survive through it.

Putting politics aside, I think of Colin Powell, who in his book "My American Journey" described how he hand painted his old used car with a brush and bucket because he could not afford to have it professionally sprayed. Yet, as a young black army soldier, survived a racially biased society to continually strive to better himself and eventually become the first African-American U.S. Secretary of State. Then there is John McCain who suffered tremendous challenges for over 5 years as a Vietnam prisoner of war and survived to one day become a Senator from Arizona and later run for President of the United States.

I also think of Nelson Mandela, who was a political prisoner for more than 27 years because he believed in freedom and equality for his people in South Africa.

Amazingly, he never gave up hope and in 1993 was given the Nobel Peace Prize. In 2010 Mandela celebrated 20 years of freedom; yet continuing to fight to have his race treated as equals with others in his country.

Then there are the extraordinary achievements of people we pass on the street who in the face of danger or personal hardships, overcome their fear to become instantaneous heros . . . pulling someone from a burning car, jumping onto the tracks of an oncoming subway train to shield a person from being hit, or interrupting the commitment of a crime.

It is virtually impossible to avoid daily news accounts of both ordinary and extraordinary events describing survivors of all types and in every part of the world. As I bring this book to close in the Fall of 2010, the people of Haiti are still facing challenges I hope to never confront, from the death and destruction caused by a major earthquake a few months ago. People along the southern coast of the United States are in despair as they watched their lives and surrounding wetlands and beaches being affected by oil gushing from a hole in the planet's crust. And countless individuals are morning the loss of loved ones in places like Iraq and Afghanistan. Obviously, there are thousands of published and unpublished accounts of such challenges and, most importantly, they all ended either in victory or defeat depending on how they were faced.

The intent of this book is squarely aimed at surviving and being victorious. As a Christian, our Bible is full of stories and analogies describing a wide range of challenges from surviving a flood, to the disciple Paul surviving his imprisonment. Other religions also have such stories. There is a ubiquitous purpose to all of this writing that should become clear to the reading audience. We learn by experience - ours or that of someone else.

Earlier, I used the words, "survive *through* the challenge". "Through" is an important point here.

Some people think that avoiding or bypassing challenges is the appropriate way to address them. This kind of thinking never works in the long run.

As an example, if you discover you are overweight, in order to lose pounds you will eventually have to cut back on your caloric intake. Sure, you can take the more drastic measure of an operation such as having the size of your stomach reduced or constricted, but this may only turn out to be a quick fix. Not surprisingly, there are individuals who have had these procedures, lost considerable weight, and then eventually overrode the effects of the operation by continuing to eat too much. They failed to address the cause of the problem - *they avoided the challenge.*

In many respects, I am no different than most of you, a somewhat ordinary person who has faced his share of challenges. I have strayed and stumbled in trying to survive God's world, failing to be faithful to my beliefs and the rules of the society in which I live, and realize there will be times in the future when faced with the same challenges, know I may not always be as strong as I should (my wife, sons, and friends often remind me of this). On the other hand, I've been privileged through my work, travels, and insatiable appetite for information to experience a wider variety of what this universe contains than most who live a more focused life. And as I've grown older, I have become wiser, more constrained, stronger in my faith, and better able to avoid temptations of my youth.

God has also granted me the ability and skill to use those experiences as a foundation for my writing and teaching. If nothing else, through my words and those of others referenced in this book, you will have the opportunity to explore challenges that may yet lie in front of you, or re-explore others you may have already experienced.

I have felt the sting of losing a job; of staying up late at night wondering how my children would do as adults; worrying about a friend who was ill; regretting not knowing my parents better; or failing to use the skills I was born with or educated to use. I have faced a war with mixed emotions; spoken to thousands about business issues that seemed important at the time that in the larger scheme of life, were not; and realized both the strength and frailty of the human spirit as others either succeeded or failed in reaching out to me when I needed their help.

Just as important is the belief that *you can and should* move forward to conquer those challenges. In order to succeed, is to believe you can do it; and another word closely related to belief is "faith". Without faith in a God that exists throughout this universe you may ultimately fail, regardless of how hard you try to succeed.

After I had finished a couple of drafts of this book, someone suggested I go back and review the Book of James in the New Testament of the Christian Bible. It is a short but meaningful read. Its verses quickly reminded me that God's challenges have been ever present with man, supporting the same theme of this book: "*. . . whenever you face trials of many kinds, . . . know that the testing of your faith will develop perseverance.*"(James 1:2). The writer continues by pointing out how we can fail through our innate tendency toward temptation, becoming attached to the values of the physical world, being deceptive, being disrespectful, just to name a few.

So here we are thousands of years later still being confronted with opportunities to fail - some brought on by ourselves and some created by others - all challenges our

God lays at our feet. It is up to us with God's assistance to find ways to survive them.

Philip Yancey, in his book, "Where is God When it Hurts", asks the question in Chapter 7, *"Is God speaking to us through our sufferings?"* I would agree with his answer of "yes". When we or someone we know is being challenged, where do we turn? Don't we ask God the big question of "why"? Why me or why them? Why now? Why should we continue? Why is this happening? Why can't I seem to do something about it?

By the fact we are turning to God, gives us a connection to his presence. In one big way, it makes us closer. It also makes us come to our sense of faith. Not only is God speaking to us at those times but we are speaking to Him. Hopefully, *we* will be "listening".

~

We always have the option to become paralyzed in thought and action. For some it destroys their lives and those around them. Others waste considerable time surveying the horizon, over-researching the situation, eventually falling hopelessly into a well of despair and frustration, constantly looking backward with little forward progress.

Once, when asked about where he stood in public opinion, Harry Truman, the 33rd President of the United States said, *"How far would Moses have gone if he had taken a poll in Egypt?"* There is certainly nothing wrong in reaching out for help and understanding, but little will be accomplished unless you believe that God expects you to move through these challenges, survive them, and become a better person for doing so.

~

The Greeks believed that their plays provided the audience a way to experience the wide range of emotions they may not otherwise have expressed openly. This "catharsis", originating from the Greek word for "cleansing" (katharsis), is often used to describe a person's ability to purge their soul by living through the actions of others. We can do the same today through our art, books, music, and movies . . . feeling fear, excitement, sadness, joy, and hope. My desire is that this book will do the same for you in a way that let's you realize God's strength to help you survive any challenge just as he has done for me and for countless others.

There is an old proverb credited to the Chinese that I heard when I was a student and goes something like this; *"To hear something is to forget; to see something is to remember; to do something is to understand."*

My hope is that you will not only see the words as they are written, but experience the stories through your mind and spirit so that you will gain a better understanding of how you can survive God's challenges.

In the hope of painting a strong mental image that will remind you of each story long after it has been read, I have sprinkled a number of facts, anecdotes, and other comments throughout the book. They should stretch your mind, provide occasional humor or pathos, and encourage you into viewing the world just a bit differently.

As you will discover, each chapter is self contained, focusing on one major challenge and covering a wide range of topics from loss of respect, to controlling anger, to losing someone close to you. Although they can be read individually in any order, Chapter I, "Crossing the Ocean", sets the stage for the remaining fourteen topics and I would recommend you begin there.

In addition, at the end of a chapter, you will find a guide to using each as the basis for individual study or group discussion with family, friends, or possibly where you worship, (as was the case when the book was being drafted). You will find a subtitle for each chapter on the "Contents" page giving you an indication of the particular chapter's focus.

I am thankful to have had the input and encouragement of several people including: my wife Ellie, many friends such as Charlie Renfroe, Chris White, Bob Day, the men at Leadership Ministries (particularly those who weathered through early drafts of the book), my oldest friend, Mike Aycox, and a teenage friend and fellow High School Yearbook staffer, and noted Christian writer, Philip Yancey.

Most of all I want to thank my God for giving me such a wonderful life even though surviving some of the challenges have been difficult and heart-wrenching at times. Yet the writing of this book has made me closer to His wisdom and those of His disciples than ever before. It has also provided me time to reflect on the "rights" and "wrongs" I have committed over the years and how I could have faced certain challenges with better morality, ethics, and wisdom if given another chance. Maybe it will do the same for you as it is read or discussed.

Even if you are not a Christian, I believe you can discover value in reading these chapters. Why? Because regardless of your faith, you will still find yourself or others you know in similar situations as described in this book. You are not alone in reaching out to your God for spiritual guidance in overcoming the various challenges. Recognize them for what they are and never lose faith in your ability to succeed.

Remember that in the bleakest of times, there is always hope. There are always fellow humans more than willing to help. And there is the spirit of God, evidenced not only in the goodness of man, but visible in the world around us if only you will stop, listen or look. You are never alone in God's universe. There are times when just a simple prayer may be all that is needed to give you the wisdom and strength to meet a particular challenge in front of you.

In summary, in many ways this book is dedicated to all of us . . . to those that have led the way before us and to those that will follow us . . . to find the right way to survive God's challenges.

It is recommended that Chapter I be read first, regardless of the order in which the others are taken.

Chapter I

CROSSING THE OCEAN

I have been lucky enough to visit Hawaii on three occasions. Besides the beauty of the separate islands that together comprise the US's fiftieth state, is a remarkable story of how they were possibly settled. For those of us who find themselves regularly cruising at over 500 miles per hour in a commercial jet, the challenge of going across half of the country in a couple of hours seems pretty simple; or getting to Hawaii from Atlanta in less than 11 hours non-stop.

If we back up a few hundred years, Christopher Columbus and his peers had a bit more of a challenge. Their ships often moved at less than 20 miles per hour, were riskier vessels in which to travel, and they certainly faced many unknowns as weather, had primitive navigation tools, and contemplated answers to such interesting questions as whether they might actually sail off the edge of the world. Yet, they weighed the risks, and obviously felt the odds *and God* was with them. Otherwise, I might not be comfortably sitting in Atlanta on a dark rainy evening, writing this book.

Imagine now, if you will, a few tops of volcanic mountains poking their heads above the surface of the vast Pacific Ocean some 1500 years ago, with no other land mass closer than roughly 2,300 miles — almost the width of the United States. Can you see yourself, along with your family and friends, packing food and belongings, climbing into a few big canoes, and saying, *"I hope there is some land past the horizon, because I just can't take living here anymore"*.

Although a bit over-simplified, that is exactly what anthropologists believe may have happened. Recent DNA tests on native Hawaiians confirm what scientists had long believed. That somewhere, about 1500-2000 years ago, a group of South Pacific Polynesians from islands north of Australia, in order to escape tribal wars and possible conflicts in religion, packed up and headed for "greener pastures". [1]

This is a truly amazing story when you consider, by faith alone, they believed they would find land, and by God's grace they somehow did discover those tops of mountains, surrounded by thousands of miles of oceans, empty except for fish and some migratory birds above. Oh, and to make it even more interesting, they carried some livestock with them, mostly pigs, and plants such as the bread fruit tree! I don't think you would find a Las Vegas odds maker willing to give even a million to one chance of there being a success in that kind of venture.

Today, can you imagine telling an entire neighborhood of people that you would like for them to paddle or sail in canoes across several thousand miles of ocean because you believe there is some really prime real estate ready for development. (Although you don't have a map showing its location, you're pretty sure land must be out there somewhere).

In another part of the world and at another time, God instructed Moses to leave the security of Egypt. To paraphrase, *"He should take all that he could carry, get all of his friends and family to do the same, and head out into the vast northeastern deserts to find a better place to live and worship . . . the "Promised Land".*

God's challenge was huge! To have his believers give up their livelihoods, many of their possessions, and risk their lives, all because of a promise . . . a challenge most of us will never know. Yet, in spite of what would appear to us as overwhelmingly negative odds, thousands of God's children not only left, but also with God's assistance, fought to leave. Sure, there were doubters, but in the end, they departed Egypt, and even more importantly, eventually succeeded in reaching that Promised Land.

~

So how difficult is it for us to make a change; to try something new; to take charge and be a leader? One way is to measure our challenge against the early Hawaiians.

To truly understand what they were up against, let's look at the logistics involved.

First, they decided to leave for lands unknown. That in itself was a big challenge and obviously was based on a belief that they could succeed. We can also assume it took a very strong leader to convince his followers it was the right thing to do. (Just think how difficult it sometimes seems loading a car full of kids and baggage and going to a vacation spot with map in hand.) Again, we don't know if that was over a period of weeks, months, or years, but you can imagine it was not overnight. And once that decision was made, a plan had to be put into effect. The logistical issues seem insurmountable. Let's do some quick calculations.

Each ocean-going canoe was estimated to be approximately 40-50 feet long; two were usually lashed together in the fashion of a modern catamaran, could carry three to four families of 4, a few pigs and some chickens. On a good day, typically without any prevailing winds in their favor, with a net forward progress of about 5 to 7 miles per hour, their canoes might travel approximately 75 miles in a 14 hour sailing day. If that pace could be maintained *continuously*, it would take 30 days to go 2300 miles, (and that assumes they went in a straight line, which again is highly unlikely). Finally, there is the issue of food and water.

An average human needs about 1 quart of water, and one pound of nourishment per day just to barely survive.[2] Thus, for a family of four, this would be 120 gallons of water (four quarts X 30 days X 4 people), and 120 pounds of food. Even if half of their food and water was obtained from rain or fishing along the way, there was still a tremendous requirement of where and how to pack the remaining supplies. Four families in a primitive catamaran would then need 290 gallons (2,370 pounds) of water and about 290 pounds of food - a huge weight and storage problem!

Oh, yes, least we forget the pigs and chickens. Even small pigs need about two pounds of nourishment per day, so for four pigs, there's another requirement of 320 pounds of food, and more water. (Luckily chickens do not require much, so their supplies can be considered negligible.)

That was a huge challenge God put before them. Yet, *they made it.*

How many tried and failed we will never know. Nor do we know how long it really took for the early adventurers to get to Hawaii. Maybe it was 15, 20, or 50 days! It certainly was not a few hours in a jet. However long, they succeeded!

~

God's challenge to Abraham as a leader, and to the Jews in his charge was as much or more of a difficult obstacle than that faced by the Hawaiians. We know that Abraham's belief in God was conveyed to his followers by both action and words . . . certainly indicative of a good leader when they have the confidence to openly communicate the situation to those that will be affected by their decisions. Unlike some leaders who are afraid of conveying the truth to their followers, Abraham let his people know what they had to do, and the risks involved.

We also know the goal for the eventual exodus of the Jewish slaves into the unknown was established when as in Ge. 17:8 God spoke to Abraham saying, *"The whole land of Canaan, where you are now an alien, I will give as an everlasting possession to you and your descendants after you."*

In a way, the desert into which Moses eventually led his followers to fulfill God's promise to Abraham, was very much like the ocean to the Hawaiians - desolate, without much water, little food, and few if any signs telling which way to go. What a tremendous challenge to place in front of so many thousands of people! And, what a better way to prove their faith to their God by accepting that challenge!

Although Moses was seen as a great leader, like most in his position, he was doubted several times, even by himself as stated in Ex. 4:1, *"What if they do not believe me or listen to me . . .?"*

Moses repeatedly told God of his doubts, and repeatedly God strengthened Moses for his role to lead. What person given such a daunting task would not have doubts in their ability. There has probably never been a General or President that has not wondered to himself whether he was making the right decision and furthermore, asked himself if he would have the confidence to lead his people based on that decision.

Harry Truman must have felt torn with emotion as he made the decision to use the atomic bomb toward the end of World War II. General Custer surely had regrets in his decision, as thousands of American Indians swarmed down the hills toward his soldiers and their eventual destruction. I feel sure as humans, all leaders have doubted their abilities or decisions, regardless of the glowing adjectives we have given their reign in our history books.

The ultimate leader for Moses of course was God. He supported him and in turn, Moses supported his followers.

This chain of support from God to us and from us to others is the way He intended our life to be - a life of reaching out, not turning inward.

Moses belief in God helped his people survive the challenges put before them, and as we should know, God never abandons those that believe in Him. On the other hand, begin worshiping the proverbial "Golden Calf" and watch what happens.

In the second book of Chronicles there is possible no better story of a leader, in this case Asa, King of Judah, making two decisions with opposite effects. As told in Chapter 14, he was confronted with overwhelming odds in a battle with an opposing army. He turned to God for support rather than to pagan or substitute beliefs as he states in verse 11, *"Lord, there is no one like you to help the powerless against the mighty. Help us, O Lord our God, for we rely on you, and in your name."* And King Asa and his army defeated the attacking force.

Moving forward to King Asa's thirty-sixth year in power, he again faced attack, but this time tried to pay off the aggressors with gold and silver by turning them against each other. And, as described in Chapter 16, although in the short run this leader's actions seemed to be a successful strategy, ultimately failed to bring lasting peace to his domain. Why? Because he was reluctant to turn to God first and tried to get another entity to confront the challenge.

Like many of us, he was full of himself, his power, his achievements, or his security. In addition, he tried to avoid facing the challenge directly.

These types of decisions have happened numerous times in the history of mankind - failing to confront challenges directly and with proper spiritual support.

Before the full involvement of the United States and others in World War II, Neville Chamberlain in 1939 tried to appease Hitler by basically ignoring pleas by the Czech Government for aid as Germany took their land. He accepted Hitler's promise interpreted as, "I won't do it again." But, just months later, in 1940, Hitler's army invaded and took the Netherlands, Belgium, and France.

Having read his address to Parliament explaining his thoughts and recommendations, it seems obvious that Chamberlain believed he was doing what was right. Yet, it is also obvious he was not willing to confront the challenge of Germany directly - something being urged by many around him. We now know his decision was a first step that, through a "domino effect", escalated Hitler's power, ego, and ultimate destruction of millions of lives.

Each of us are put in situations where we must either lead or get out of the way. And if we choose to lead, are we prepared to be a good leader, or bad leader? In other words, is our heart true and honest or are we motivated to guide our followers based on mortal temptations as greed or ego? Even gangs of thugs and robbers have leaders, evil as they may be.

Like many of you, I have found myself questioning decisions about a job or expense that would certainly impact my family. Would I be worthy of leading them if I did not take the time to consider the repercussions of my actions?

Do I have the intellectual acumen and spiritual spine to stand up and move forward?

Will I become frozen in fear because of self doubts and weakness of soul?

Am I in tune with God, or playing the song of life off key?

All are questions we can face, and more importantly, answer positively, *if we are properly prepared*! Instead of planning and preparing for many of life's hurdles, we wander through our day-to-day existence never considering how we will act until faced with the event. Then we find ourselves confused or fearful of the decisions we might make. Moreover, in our haste to do something, often we fail to realize the relative severity of the challenge and react inappropriately.

~

How trivial some of our so-called challenges seem to be in comparison to those faced by Moses and the children of Israel, or those early wanderers that founded Hawaii. Today, we find ourselves worried about moving to another state to take a new job, or wringing our hands when our children leave for college. We allow self-created stress to cause premature heart attacks, react with insanity to less than insane situations, or ruin perfectly good relationships by allowing ourselves to be mislead by others.

Yes, maybe they do seem like big, earthshaking events at the time, but are they really that much of a challenge? Only a few generations back, some of our own ancestors packed up and headed across oceans to other continents, or hitched horses to a wagon and walked or rode their way thousands of miles for greener pastures and promised riches. Weren't those greater challenges? Where would a country like the United States, Canada, or Australia be if it had not been for the brave and courageous people who traveled to and populated those lands, buoyed by their conviction of faith and belief in God?

Even more recently, thousands have sought political or economic refuge from countries like Vietnam, Haiti, the Sudan, and Cuba. In desperation, often risking their lives, they left their friends and relatives, possibly never to see them again. Have you ever done something like that? Could you?

Ask yourself how many towns, or cross-road communities, have the name "Hope" or "New Hope"?

After a little research through the Internet, it seems that most states in the US and many countries have at least one if not several. For Georgia, my home state, there appears to be a minimum of seven. Obviously, someone or some group believed so much in a better future, they selected the name to symbolize a new start, a "new hope". In contrast, searching the Internet revealed no town or community named "Hopeless".

~

For the early Hawaiian voyagers, and for Moses' followers, I firmly believe God's hand was instrumental to both groups' success. And, I also believe God can be instrumental to us surviving the daily challenges that are part of our lives. In one form or another, they are inescapable. All we have to do is believe in Him and ask for guidance. He will put all things in perspective. As God said to Moses, Ex. 15:13, *"In your unfailing love you will lead . . . In your strength you will guide them . . ."*

Great leaders are forged and tempered by surviving great challenges.

Vaclav Havel, became the leader and President of Czecho-slovakia in 1989 and later President of the Czech Republic in 1993, after successfully overcoming suppressed criticism of the Communist rule that dominated his country for decades. Although imprisoned several times, he never gave up his fight for democracy. As a writer and playwright, he used his talent to openly criticize the government. And, although offered sanctuary outside of his country, he stayed, believing he had to find solutions and help his citizens heal from within. After his election, in a speech he stated, *"I want to be a President that will speak less and work more."* His work, not talk, freed millions to be able to determine their own future, again believe in the strength of the individual, and, most importantly, worship as they pleased.

Great leaders are remembered for what they did and not what they said.

Whether you are a parent, or sibling, a teacher, a doctor, a lawyer, or bricklayer, with faith you *can* lead through all challenges, with less worry. And you will do so with a greater perspective of what really matters in your life, and an understanding of the true magnitude of the challenges you will inevitable face.

All of us have the ability to lead our family, friends, business associates, or even people we do not know across the unknown waters or deserts of our future. And like the Hawaiians and the Children of Israel, *by faith we can survive and succeed!*

Study Guide – Chapter I
Crossing the Ocean

This first chapter sets the stage for each of the others in the book. Because of that fact, this chapter's study guide relates to the entire issue of challenge and is a good beginning point for self-examination or group discussion. You may find yourself or your group coming back to this first study after you have read subsequent chapters to see if there has been any changes to the answers you would give.

Because we face challenges of all types every day (even getting out of bed may be the first each morning), try and identify what you may remember to be the top three that you have experienced. List each one and then rank them in order beginning with the greatest challenge being number one.

Now consider each of the following:

1. Did the challenge seem greater when it occurred than it does now when you think about it? If so, why do you believe your perception has changed?

2. Do you think you will see the most recent challenge differently a few years from now, and if so, why?

3. How did you overcome each challenge? Did you have assistance? Did you turn to other people or God or both? What type of comfort did you get from each?

When you still lived with your parents or guardian, did you ever experience moving to a different city or country (or maybe having to change schools or live in a different neighborhood)? If you haven't had those experiences, use your imagination to answer each of the following:

4. What caused the greatest anxiety – list each (an example would be "loss of friends"). Reviewing the book of "Exodus" in the Bible beginning with the 6th Chapter, 1-12, what caused Moses' greatest anxiety as he anticipated leaving Egypt?

5. After your move, list all of the benefits or positive points that resulted because of the change. In retrospect, was the move a good thing? Explain why or why not.

6. Did someone help you in seeing the positive points that could result from the move? If so, how did they approach the subject and did it help? Did God do the same for Moses?

When faced with another challenge in the future, honestly answer each of the following from your perspective:

7. Do you believe it is a sign of weakness to reach out for help? Why or why not?

8. Would you rather turn to God for help or to another person? Explain your answer.

9. Has prayer helped you overcome one or more of the top three challenges you listed above?

After you have completed this study, would you re-rank the list or keep it the same? If you would re-rank the challenges, explain why?

Finally, now that you have done the exercises, did it cause you to think of other challenges that may have been greater? If so, start the study again using the new challenges you have remembered!

Group Discussion

1. In listening to other members discuss what they thought was their greatest challenge, do your challenges seem more or less significant? Explain.

2. Did you learn of a way that may assist you at overcoming a challenge in the future? Express this to the others.

3. Is there someone in your group that epitomizes the kind of leadership you admire? Explain to the group your position?

4. List and discuss the traits of leadership that Jesus exemplified giving specific examples.

5. When are the times and/or where are the places when the action of a group may provide greater or more sustained leadership as compared to an individual? Was there an instance in the New Testament where this happened?

Chapter II

A PRECIOUS LOSS

On March 22, 2002, I placed my hand on the head of our family's English Springer Spaniel as he lay on an examination table in the doctor's office. And then, along with my wife, gently stroked his soft fur as our vet administered a drug that placed him into a sleep from which he would never awaken. Thus ended his life-long relationship with my wife, our two boys, and me . . . fourteen years which seemed all too short for us, but as the doctor said, a long life for him.

During the last two years he had rapidly become feeble, was almost blind, and could hear only the loudest of sounds, although on good days (with some assistance) he could still locate his tennis ball by smell alone. In the winter months preceding that day in March, other health problems complicated his day-to-day existence and so, as a family, we made the dreaded decision to have him put to sleep.

March in Georgia can mean cold blustery days just above freezing or wonderfully warm spring afternoons with little wind. For our friend Simon, this was one of the nicer days. For a few hours before we took him to the vet, I led him on his leash slowly up and down the street in front of our house where he once barked and romped after cars and kids on bikes. After awhile I sat in the pine straw at the edge of a field nearby and rubbed his back in the warm sun. I know this was more for me than for him as I collected the memories of his antics with the children, particularly our oldest boy who had grown to manhood during Simon's short life on earth. And of course, I remembered those embarrassing times when he barked when he shouldn't or innocently chased after a jogger.

As a breed, Springers are very energetic, calm a bit with age, and are usually even dispositioned around most people. In fact, Simon accommodated two family cats that, for some reason, decided he made a great mattress on cold winter nights. Above all though, he was true to his family and dearly loved by us.

On a relative scale of approximately 7 human years to each dog year, canines are into their "teen years" in less than 24 months, and Simon at 14 was equivalent to about an 84 year-old man. Each of God's creatures has a predetermined life clock that varies from species to species and there is little we can do to change it. There are Galapagos turtles that are plodding the ground in the 21st Century that were alive during the American Civil War. There are bald eagles that have soared above the Alaskan wilderness since the 1970's. And there are elephants that bore the weight of Asian soldiers in World War II, that are still beasts of burden at the beginning of the 21st century. Yet, in the few hours it has taken to write this chapter, thousands of other creatures have been born and later died of old age.[3]

Research has shown many influencing factors on life spans of all living creatures including man.

High carbon intake in diets (the same carbon molecules on burned meat or what causes caramel to be brown) can impair cells from reproducing at a normal rate and thus cause premature aging. Early exposure during the first months of life to certain bacteria in our environment apparently strengthens an animal's life-long immune response making them less likely to fall suspect to disease or having problems like asthma. Decreases in stress lowers the oxidation levels within animal cells, increasing the life expectancy of the cells and thus the life of the creature. But, regardless of countless other factors as these, so far man has not been able to alter the inevitable conclusion to life, as we know it. We would have liked for Simon to be with us always, but it just wasn't meant to be.

~

There are different levels of attachment we make in life. One set of attachments to our family, another to friends, one type for fellow workers, a different type for our pets, and even attachments to inanimate objects like cars or books or old pieces of furniture. (Some, known as "hoarders" become so obsessively connected to "stuff", they have trouble parting with virtually everything). What many of us find difficult is drawing the line between those different types of relationships and realizing which ones are truly important and those that are of lesser value. I think some, if not most of this delineation of values must come from the heart and not the mind.

Having spent the much of my career in sales or marketing, I know most purchases are not made on logical assessments of a product's functions but rather on a *vision* of what they could possibly do for, or provide to, the buyer. It is a rare person that evaluates and procures a car based on the quality of the engine, strength of the transmission, or thickness of the sheet metal . . . all very objective and worthwhile measures. More often they will select a car based on the overall look, the color, the feeling of the upholstery, the sound system, placement of cup holders, or, (whether they want to admit it or not), the "statement" it will make when they pull into the driveway.

We find ourselves trying to live a life of perception rather than reality. We make emotionally driven decisions rather than logically facing the truth.

People, pets, and objects like the car, inherit those emotions. They build up or diminish over time depending on our relationship to them. Why else would we ever sell that wonderful car we bought after only three or four years if it were not for the fact that we somehow fell out of "love" with it? Or, in other words, maybe it no longer satisfied our emotional need . . . not fast enough, not big enough, or not as pretty as the newer models. In a way, our "throwaway" society, particularly in the United States, has led to other types of throwaway relationships; and not just relationships to objects, but to people, to marriages, to companies, and in some cases, our faith.

~

Simon was not just a dog, he was part of our living family. He was not an investment we made because of his pedigree, but rather he was an investment of the heart.

I once heard a preacher talk about investments in relationships. *"Much like investing in a deposit account at the bank"*, he said, *"we can also invest of ourselves in others. And like the bank account, over time our investment in people will build credit, and compound itself in growth that far surpasses any physical asset in which we could ever invest. The more we put in, the more we will get out in return."*

What he said is true. Those investments in the living are the most important investments we can ever make. That's why it is so difficult to lose those relationships, even when that inevitable time comes, either through natural causes, or war, a self-inflicted injury, an act of violence, or accident.

Many of you know of situations where a loved one was injured in an accident and all normally monitored vital signs indicated that their brain had ceased to function. For all intensive purposes, only the living tissue of the body remained, artificially keep alive by modern marvels of our medical industry. Like many, I believe that once the brain "dies", the spirit and soul of that person has left their human form. Yet many relatives choose to keep the body living for days or months in hope that something will change . . . the person they love will return. Although I pray I will never face that situation, my faith tells me I will be able to make the right decision if it were to occur.

Paul, in his letter to the church of Corinth, at the very beginning of 2 Corinthians (1:3-7), starts with statements intended to comfort those Christians trying to hold on to their beliefs as they were being besieged by non-believers, doubters within their ranks, and by physical abuse from others. And buried within that section is the phrase, *"Jesus Christ . . . the God of all comfort, who comforts us in all our troubles, so that we can comfort those in any trouble"*.

One of the times we as humans need comforting the most is when we have to face the mortality of a living being.

When my father was in his fifties, he had a stroke while having a medical test. I still remember the first night at the hospital when I spoke with the nurse about the situation. I'm not sure if it was the emotional strain of the situation, a lack of supper, or just the heat of a hot summer day in a car without air conditioning for the previous hour, but I almost fainted. It's the only time in my life that has ever happened.

I remember a close neighbor who was also a nurse, sitting in the waiting room and telling me to sit down and put my head between my knees as she noticed I was wobbly and sweating profusely. As I sat there, I wondered if I would ever see my father alive again, or if he would die in intensive care before being allowed visitors. And if he did not die, how would the stroke affect him?

For most, the challenge of confronting death will be in front of us many times. We cannot run away from it or hide behind shields made of unrealistic hopes that death will go away. However, in all situations we can pray for guidance and know that God can bear our burden with us. As the writer of Psalm 23 states in verse 4, *"Even though I walk through the valley of the shadow of death, I will fear no evil, for you are with me; your rod and your staff, they comfort me."* What a wonderful analogy of strength of the shepherding God to us as his sheep. It is the theme of a wonderful little book written by Mary Glynn Peeples, someone I have met on several occasions. It is titled, "All We Like Sheep." In it she constantly paints a picture of how God helps us overcome our weaknesses, just as the shepard does the same for their flock of sheep. It is an analogy as strong today as it was thousands of years ago as depicted in the Bible.

We also need to realize that becoming detached from the living body is not becoming detached from their spirit.

The strength of our faith should hold our ties to them for eternity and our memories of them should bring joy to our lives rather than sadness to our hearts.

We need to remember what was, rather than what could have been.

And most important, *we need to move forward with our lives.* As one attachment is physically broken, should we not immediately seek to make others or strengthen the ones we have?

Intentionally leaving an emotional void in your heart for a loved one who has died serves no purpose. As proof, there are many examples in the Bible where the loss of a spouse was eventually followed by marriage to a new partner. Even Abraham, after the loss of his wife Sarah, his companion for many decades, married again at a very old age and had children by his new wife Keturah. Was his new wife a surrogate for Sarah? Of course not. She did, however, fill a void by making him whole again; by providing the kind of physical and emotional attachment only a spouse can give.

For man, it seems we need emotional completeness to be healthy. Without it, we often become mentally and physically weak. Research has shown that a loving attachment to other living creatures gives us a greater chance of having a longer and happier life. It helps mend the emotional bond that was broken by the death of someone close to us.

In my situation, if my wife were to die before me, I believe she would want me to remarry. Similarly, I would certainly want her to do the same if I died first (but to someone not quite as handsome as me). I think we both would want to restore our emotional well-being and taking another partner could be part of the prescription.

Not being able to emotionally reconnect or to remain wallowing in sorrow after the death of a loved one, not only can be unhealthy, it can be destructive to other relationships. I have experienced three situations in which the death of a family member broke the bonds that had previously held them together.

The first happened when I was in my mid-twenties after the wife of a person with whom I worked accidentally ran over their only son. As I remember it, their young teenager had been sharing rides on a scooter. In between trips he had waited by lying on the family's driveway, in what turned out to be a blind spot just below a sharp rise at the entrance. His mom came back from a trip, pulled into the driveway and not being able to see her son, rolled over him, taking his life. In less than a year the parents divorced.

Another family I became acquainted with about fifteen years ago, lost their only son when gasoline being poured into a lawnmower was ignited by a gas water heater located in their garage. The house was totally destroyed and the boy died a few days later from his burns. Even with the strong support of family, friends and church, several years later the couple went their separate ways.

Finally, a person I have known since the late 1990's, lost one of his two son's as a casualty of the 9-11 attack. He was a rising star at Cantor Fitzgerald, the trading firm that occupied the top floors of the 1 World Trade Center building. The organization lost a total of 658 employees that morning in 2001.[4] After struggling to accept what had happened, he and his wife also divorced a few years later but remain as friends.

Words like "devastating" barely begin to describe these situations. I've asked myself how would I act if one of my boys were to die and hope my faith along with the support of those who care about our family would carry us through the challenge. Although there appears to be a mythical statistic indicating between 75-90% of families with such a loss end in divorce, in reality some surveys thankfully indicate it is far less.

One recent study conducted in 2006 by an organization called, "The Compassionate Friends" indicates the rate may be closer to 16%, still a high number. Obviously there are many factors that influence the actual percentage, none the less being the support provided by family, friends, their place of worship, and the relationship the parents had before the death of the child.

For those who will face this type of loss, we can guide them in two directions.

First, they can turn to their God, and to the basis of their faith for immediate support. As a Christian I can pick up a copy of my Bible and re-read the stories of calamities that inflicted death into families over many centuries and how they were resolved.

Second, I can seek out people who have survived past these types of personal losses and ask for their guidance. Organizations familiar to us like MADD[5] (Mothers Against Drunk Drivers) is an example of many groups dedicated to helping people survive the challenge of a personal loss. Some are universal in nature while others focus on a particular relationship: a child, a parent, a sibling, etc. Whatever you do, don't be afraid or embarrassed to reach out for help.

~

My father did recover from the stroke. It caused him to give up smoking and to even lose a few pounds. Although he had some minor lasting effects, he lived another fifteen years to see the birth of his four grand children and long enough for them to know him.

Take a moment each day and isolate your thoughts to those important relations you have now or have had in the past . . . to the living world around you. Appreciate the "Simons" in your life, the neighbors or fellow workers that you have shared laughter with, the memories of childhood friends playing in the fields or streets of your town, or the joy of walking with someone you care about.

If you believe these thoughts are what you want to have more of, then create more of those experiences. Turn off the TV and talk to your spouse or children; get off the sofa and instead of watching a game, be in one; or walk across the street and spend time getting to know your neighbor! Don't just agree with this statement, do something about it . . . now!

There was a recent television ad that began by showing a man playing with his dog. Then the man gets a high speed connection to his computer through the telephone company that sponsored this advertisement. Sadly, the commercial promotes the fact that after getting his new service the man is able to spend much of his time on the computer surfing the Internet while his dog is mostly ignored. Where were the hearts and minds of the creators, producers, and executives that made and approved this advertisement? This kind of warped thinking is evident throughout our society.

Although we've had cats, turtles, spiders, fish, hamsters, rabbits, and a multitude of other ephemeral creatures, Simon was our first *family* pet. We will always remember him as he is in a painting with our boys . . . tongue hanging out, eyes bright, and a look that said, *"throw the ball, quick, before I have a panic attack!"*

Our faith in what was right and best for Simon led us to a very specific decision that we carried out *for him* on that day in March, even though our emotional attachment was very strong. We had to have faith that what we were doing was in his best interest and not ours. In Isa 7:9 God states, " . . . *If you do not stand firm in your faith, you will not stand at all.*"

Facing a life and death situation is a great challenge and I admire the doctors, nurses, medics, and others who see it day after day. It takes a special person to do this and we should all be grateful for their dedication. My youngest son Ty recently completed five years in the Navy as a Corpsman providing medical support to the ¼ Marines out of Camp Pendleton, California. During two tours in combat areas of Iraq, he saw the devastation to human life caused by war. I admire him for his service more than he will every know. With faith in God and through the support of those we know or know of us, we can get past this type of life or death challenge.

There is certainly room for both logic and emotion in our lives, and by faith we can use both wisely to make the right decisions for those we love . . . in life and in death.

Study Guide – Chapter II
A Precious Loss

Facing the death of someone close to you can be one of the most difficult challenges in life and usually one that is repeated over and over again. Likewise, the loss of any of God's creatures for which you have created an emotional bond can also be a traumatic event.

Think of someone you have known well and who is no longer living. Then answer the following questions:

1. If you had to select only one word to describe that person, what would it be and why?

2. Select from the following list, which word best describes how you felt when they died, and then write a one sentence explanation as to why you picked that word -

- Sadness

- Guilt

- Remorse

- Loneliness

- Anger

- Fear

- Relief

- Frustration

3. If you could sit and talk with them for just one hour the day before they died, what would you discuss? Is there one sentence you would like to say to them? Is there one sentence your would like for them to say to you?

4. *When you last communicated with them before they died, what was the tone of the conversation (even if in a written form like a letter or email)?*

5. *If given the opportunity, would you have changed anything relative to your relationship and why? Do you think telling them through prayer would help?*

Before answering the next set of questions, think of those people with whom you currently interface (relatives, friends, co-workers, etc.). If one or more of them were to die unexpectedly in the near future, consider the following:

6. *Would you be satisfied with your existing relationship at that point in time? If you answered no, then what would you change before they died?*

7. *List at least three individuals and describe how you might change your relationship to them if you knew they would die tomorrow? Now that you have made the list, shouldn't you get in touch with them before it is too late?*

Group Discussion

1. *From question "2" above, have each member of the group pick one person and the corresponding word that best described how they felt and have them explain their selection. Try and cover as many of the words as possible by asking members to think of individuals that might fit a specific emotional feeling listed.*

2. *Have each group member pick one relationship they believe needs "repairing". Try and get a commitment from the group member to contact that individual as soon as possible and report the results back to the group, at the next meeting.*

3. Discuss the positive aspects of getting assistance from others when someone loses a person close to them.

4. When Jesus knew he was to die, how did he try to strengthen his relationships? (Read John 13:12)

5. Are friendships different today than they might have been when Jesus lived? Why or why not? (Consider the foundations on which friendships are built.)

6. There are two important aspects when we talk about someone's background - demographics and psychographics. Look up the definition of each and then discuss how or if either of the two could influence friendships.

Chapter III

BEING RUN OVER

Will Rogers is quoted as saying *"Even if you're on the right track, you'll get run over if you just sit there."* With just a little bit of thought, it's easy to see how that statement can be applied to many circumstances. For me, it was being caught on the wrong end of a downturn in the economy.

Like many folks, the high tech bubble that burst in 2000 directly affected my billfold. Having been in the software and services industry for about two-thirds of my working life, I had seen the rise and fall of many technology-oriented companies. Some had been built on strong financial foundations with sound business models and experienced leadership. Others were constructed on "get-rich-dreams" as evidenced by all of the dot com companies that went to market at the end of the twentieth century. And whether you were employed in the industry, a direct investor, or had your retirement funds tied to some of those companies, many folks suffered financially.

In February 2000, I took the plunge and left one of the world's largest companies to go to work for a start-up organization of less than 100 people (big by some standards). And although they propositioned a good product, the temptation to make "millions" through the thousands of stock options they hung in front of me was the deciding factor to go to work there. The bottom line . . . it was a greed motivated decision.

Some will remember that in April 2000, less than 60 days after beginning the trek to make my quick fortune, the stock market began its downward slide (it was two years and counting when I started this book). My mother always had a favorite expression, *"It's like showing up to the sale, a day late and a dollar short"*. Well, I was definitely a "day late" and after 12 months found myself not only with fewer dollars than I anticipated, but was jumping on board with yet another company.

As an officer in the sales organization, I immediately began putting in the requisite 10-12 hour days, and after a few months found my group successfully moving toward increases in contracted revenue greater than 60% over the previous year. And except for the occasional bump, I thought I had parked myself on a track that seemed secure. Little did I know others in the organization were on a collision course with my "train", nor did I notice the financial crossties holding the rails were falling out.

I'm not sure if God was giving me a wake-up call by having me confront the reality of being unemployed, or whether I was just overdue. Regardless, with the company teetering on the point of bankruptcy, and management principles contrary to my own, the result was my resignation being coerced from me after only nine, of what I thought, very successful months.

Many people may never know the various feelings that you can face after losing a job. One person said, *"Ya know, when it happened to me once, it was like a death in the family. There was a period of grieving, of remembrance, some regrets, and then, after some time passed, I was able to move forward with my life."*

That's not a bad analogy!

Whether the loss of a job is your fault, the company's, or just a poor economic environment that affects many people at once, it is still a challenge that has to be overcome. What we have to be very careful not to do is drown in a pool of blame, BUT we do need to always analyze what has happened, beginning with ourselves.

One of my favorite sets of verses in the New Testament of the Bible is in Matthew 7:1-5. The section is devoted to judging others, and in particular, verse 3 states, *"Why do you look at the speck of sawdust in your brother's eye and pay no attention to the plank in your own eye?"*

Was I fully or partially to blame for my loss of employment? Could I have better prepared for what now seems an inevitable consequence of events? Did I place trust in the wrong people? Was I fair to my employer? Did I continually ask for God's guidance?

At the suggestion of an old business acquaintance, I partnered with another person I had known for twenty years to fill the income void both of us were facing in the early 2000's. Not being able to find a job in the technology field, we relied on manual skills we both had in construction to help make mortgage payments. From building custom cabinets, to trimming out an entire house, we stayed busy for several years until the job market turned around - a long way from the six-figure salaries we had at one time.

The low point for me came one day when a lady where we were doing some carpentry work asked me to crawl under her house to put wire over a hole where her cat had been escaping. About half-way there on my belly, covered with Georgia red clay, an abandoned pipe that I was under dumped years of old, cold, rancid water on me. My chin on the ground for at least 30 seconds, I thought, *"Do I stop, or do I go on?"* I went on. Later when the smell of my clothes almost made my wife leave the house when I came in that evening, I was able to have a good laugh.

Going on . . . that's what we must all do.

31

If we spend a few moments looking into the mirror for the speck(s) in our eye, maybe we can find a way to keep them from getting in there again (or at least find better goggles). More importantly, we can move forward past this challenge, because in the greater scheme of life, that's all it really is . . . a test by God to see how we will do.

As is often quoted, *"In hindsight you always have 20/20 vision."* Those of us who are sports enthusiasts often find ourselves doing Monday morning "quarterbacking". It's easy to discuss what was done right or wrong for a particular game play. If we just spent as much time thinking about what we could have done better at our job, or for our employer, or fellow worker, could we not use that 20/20 vision to improve everyone's chance for success. Ask yourself the question, *"am I employed because I like the company and the people, and I feel like I am a contributor to everyone's success, or, am I there just for the benefit of myself?"*

~

During 1932, many newspapers printed the government's statistics of unemployment that reached an all time high of 23.6%. Basically, one out of every four available workers were without a job. It was not until 1941, that the wartime economy took unemployment in the United States under 10%.

Today, as I do the final editing of this book in the fall of 2010, the jobless rate is hovering above 9%. Is this as terrible as many people seem to think? Absolutely not! Are there thousands of jobs going unfilled? Absolutely, yes! There are always jobs to be done, even in 1932.

Being unemployed only seems like a terrible situation if you think of it that way. Statistics indicate that many of today's most successful businesses were born from necessity when someone found themselves without a job. If you find yourself unemployed, then the quickest way to move forward is first to get re-employed with God and best of all, this is a job that you can keep for life. His perfect vision for us is always clear.

I believe that a change in a job (whether prompted by you or initiated by someone else) can always lead to something better. Look at the disciples of Christ. Many like Paul and Peter made dramatic career changes. Can you imagine being trained as a fisherman, a skill usually passed down for generations, and then one day decide to do something entirely different. And because of that change in jobs, affect the lives of millions for generations to come?

~

My "greedy" move to a startup company got me away from a huge organization with questionable sales tactics. And although with the little organization only a year, the experience taught me a lot about the Internet, a force that is rapidly shaping our way of learning, communicating, and doing business. Did I gain the monetary wealth I had gone after? No! But more importantly, I gained a wealth of knowledge that I will always have. I also gained a friend for life, who, in my time of employment need has been a guardian angel. Both the knowledge and friendship are more important than all the stock options in the world.

Was my next nine-month career as rewarding and secure as I had expected? Unfortunately, the answer is no. But again, I was able to do something more important. I rescued two great salespeople from the ranks of unemployment. One I had known both as a boss, and peer, and the other, a young man who had been highly recommended by a long time business friend. Those are two accomplishments of which I can always be proud and are certainly more inwardly rewarding.

Surviving the loss of a job, even if it is your own proprietorship that has failed, is always achievable.

*Instead of thinking about probabilities of failure,
think about possibilities of success.*

When you lose a job, sometimes, (or even *most* times), it's
hard to stay positive.

~

You might be surprised to discover how many of the great
leaders of the past and present began by losing one or
more jobs.

Arthur Blank, presently owner of the Atlanta Falcons and
benefactor to several multi-million dollar community projects, along with fellow worker, Bernie Marcus was fired
by one company in 1978, only to pick themselves up and
found Home Depot in 1979 —- one of the most successful
retail companies of all time. Even though they lost over $1
million on sales of $7 million that first year, they were
profitable the next and each year thereafter, today em-
ploying over 300,000 associates at over 2200 stores glob-
ally.[6]

Many men nearing 50 years old, would have given up,
thinking more of retiring than starting a new company.
But instead, Arthur Blank's and Bernie Marcus' vision
and confidence led them to take their experience and build
a better mouse trap.

Another retailer named "Bernie" (better known as Barney), several generations earlier, faced repeated challenges, any one of which could have caused him throw in
the towel, to give up.

Coming from a strong and strict Christian home, his
mother made him quit his first job because he was required to work on Sundays. Barney's choice was to take a
job on a farm almost 30 miles away. Unfortunately, he al-

most died from malaria, forcing him to return home and get a job at the Northern and Pacific Tea Company. However, a few months later, he lost his employment when the company's profits began a rapid decline.

After a couple of other unsuccessful jobs, he and a friend opened their own store called "The Great Western Tea Company" but within just weeks of beginning their business, their only horse that pulled the delivery wagon was hit and killed by a train. Barney barely missed being killed himself because he was the driver of that wagon. Then a short time later his brother died and Barney had to handle the funeral expenses, almost breaking him financially. Surely disappointed, he could have quit but instead he trudged on still with the belief he would succeed.

Just when things seemed to be getting better, the Ohio river flooded his store destroying most of his inventory. But Barney just would not give up and with perseverance and support from the admiring community, by 1902 he had 40 stores and changed the business marquee to incorporate the now familiar title of his last name, to, "The *Kroger* Company". When he died in 1938 at the age of 78, he had established one of the best known names in the retail grocery business which still continues strong today.[7]

~

What if you had a job but were physically restrained from doing it?

In a way, being stopped from using your God given talent is almost like losing your job. This is certainly what Paul confronted as described in the Bible.

In the New Testament, Paul is deprived of his mission by being imprisoned by the Romans. On the surface it would appear he has been robbed of his duties, unable to fulfill what he sees as his responsibility.

Some might think that being in jail would be the end of their ability to perform any meaningful work. Yet, in his letter to the followers of Christ in Philippi (which forms the basis for the book of "Philippians"), instead of considering his imprisonment an impediment, he uses it to promote his faith. Instead of being down spiritually, he writes with an uplifted voice!

Remarkably, Paul looks at adversity and sees only victory. In Philippians 1:12 he says, *"Now I want you to know, brothers, that what has happened to me has really served to advance the gospel."* In other words, *"hey folks, don't look at what has happened to me as being a problem, but rather consider it another way to further Christ's word."*

Later in respect to his plight, Paul references the increased outspokenness of others who preach the word of Christ, and writes, *"The important thing is that in every way, whether from false motives or true, Christ is preached. And because of this I rejoice".*

This book in the Bible - this letter from Paul - is one of the purest forms of encouragement ever put to words. It tells of a man who has his employment with God interrupted only through the physical constraints of prison, but never interrupted spiritually. It is the story of someone who takes what most would see as a hopeless situation and makes it into one of hope.

Most importantly, Paul is able to put into perspective the value of faith over all problems when at the end of 4:12 he begins, *"I have learned the secret of being content in any and every situation, whether well fed or hungry, whether living in plenty or in want. I can do everything through him who gives me strength".*

When the economy has a downturn, many people take jobs that under-employ their talents. Over time they often allow their situation to cause resentment to those around them or toward those that employ them.

On one hand we take the job because we need the income, while at the same time blaming them for giving us a job that seems beneath our abilities. Aren't we biting the hand that feeds us? Where is our thankfulness for getting the job? Are we a better person than those with lesser jobs? And is it below our dignity to take such a position?

I am reminded of the movie, "No Time For Sergeants", a comedy in which the American actor, Andy Griffith, plays a World War II draftee who enters the army as an under-educated country "bumpkin". His sergeant, wanting to make sure he is not an embarrassment to the company, places him in charge of the barracks's latrine (bathroom). Not only does the private not realize that he has been given a demeaning assignment, he works as hard as he can to do the best with the task at hand.

Hour after hour Griffith cleans and polishes every knob, piece of chrome, sinks, woodwork and all of the other hardware in the latrine. When an officer arrives to inspect the barracks, the private is given high praise for the cleanliness and then he returns the officer's salute by causing all of the toilet seats to rise in unison. It was the private's intention to do this out of respect and not as a joke. As funny as this was, it reminds us of an important point.

We should always try and do the best job we can, even when we are not employed doing the greater tasks we believe we are capable of doing.

Think of unemployment as a great opportunity to do something new. Even if you are happily employed, encourage those that are not. Keep all options open . . . start a company, dramatically change careers, go back to school, fix

all those things that have been neglected (including relationships), become a full-time volunteer, or . . . maybe
even write a book!

Study Guide – Chapter III
Being Run Over

We make career changes for all types of reasons. Sometimes it is to do something our heart desires, to fulfill a dream, or to challenge ourselves to do more with our life. In other instances the choice is made for us.

In Bob Buford's book, "Half-Time", he felt compelled to have a second career . . . to do something more with his life in a truly meaningful way. In studying his book many years back, it became evident to me there is certainly many more aspects to life than the accumulation of fortune and fame.

In thinking about what life may bring you or what you may bring to life, consider the following:

1. Do you believe your current occupation provides the best use of your skills and if not, why?

2. If you are dissatisfied with your "job", what are you doing positively to change the situation? (if you are satisfied, then list three reasons why).

3. If you could select any job, what would it be and how would you get to that occupation? Do you plan to do something to make that happen, and if not, why?

4. List two disciples of Jesus and explain why they left their previous occupations to follow him?

5. Have you ever followed someone you knew or worked for into another career or company? If so, why did you make the change and was it eventually decided it was the right choice? Explain.

Assuming you or someone you knew changed jobs primarily for monetary reasons:

6. Was your (their) life improved or were there problems as a result of the new job?

7. If you (they) devoted more time to the new job responsibilities, were other sacrifices made and if so, what were they?

Group Discussion

1. Has anyone in your group benefitted by having their career changed by someone other than themselves (being fired, put on furlough, losing a job by the all-too-prevalent R.I.F.[8]*)? Have them describe the situation.*

2. Ask group members to relate situations where they were forced to make a career change they had not planned. Where did they seek support?

3. Ask each member to answer the question, "If you could not continue your current job or profession with any similar business, starting tomorrow, what skills could you take to another organization?"

4. Has anyone in your group recently lost their job, and if so, how did other members help them through the experience?

5. Ask each member to relate an experience where they have helped another person get a job by describing the situation the individual was in prior to getting the new position (depressed, financially weak, upbeat, alone, hopeless, positive, etc.)

6. Discuss a time when Jesus may have felt abandoned and how the situation was resolved.

Chapter IV

RESPECTIVELY YOURS

In a world that is commoditized, pre-packaged, shrink-wrapped, and mass-marketed, there is a value that can never be bought or sold. It is "respect". You can strip away all other human attributes or adjectives to describe someone, and in the final analysis they could still have respect; but the real question is, *"will they be respected?"*

Gaining and holding respect is a tremendous challenge. I sometimes feel God gives us respect, in order to take it away and then see how (and if) we will work to regain it.

Acquiring respect is hard; losing respect is easy.

A long time friend, Rick Page, who started a very successful sales training organization and authored a popular book called "Hope is not a Strategy", often stated, *"it only takes one aw shucks, to offset a whole bunch of attaboys"*. I believe the same can be paraphrased for respect.

One violation of integrity, one blatant act breaking a sacred commandment or one foolish slip of the tongue can destroy years of respect that we may have placed in another individual or institution. Obviously, the same can happen to each of us if we do not constantly monitor how we act as a part of the human family and, more importantly, as children of God.

How many times in recent history have we seen authority figures as Ministers, Rabbis, Teachers or Politicians - people holding highly regarded positions - lose the respect of their followers by committing an act that betrays their faith or oath? And how many times have we followed the lives of famous athletes into oblivion because of weaknesses in their moral fiber? And, how unfortunate it is that our youth, all too often influenced by those same figureheads, must witness the loss of integrity, losing their innocence of trust and respect in those they once admired. It is no wonder today that our young are skeptical of their leaders and look very hard at their parents for steadfastness.

Our newly elected President Obama is an example of our nation wanting a change from the perceived status quo of government; reaching out to someone with charisma and a stated purpose of making a change. Only time will tell if he is able to fulfill his promises or if he falls to political temptations and loss of respect as so many that have gone before him.

Is this some new phenomenon?

Daryl Strawberry is the epitome of someone who was one of those rare individuals endowed with athletic abilities well beyond most mortals. Beginning his professional baseball career in 1983 he was selected as Rookie of the Year. Over his 16 years in and out of baseball he was voted to the All-Star roster 8 times and holds the record of being the only player chosen the first five consecutive years he was eligible. Able to hit home runs with ease, he was unfortunately unable to easily avoid drugs and violence.

Early in his career, fans cheered when he made his first comeback from a bout from drugs - hoping for the best from such a rising and gifted ball player. Today, many still hold him in disrespect, however it now appears he has turned his life around, frequently giving talks about the hope he has derived from addiction treatment.[9]

There have been others who have set poor examples as well like Mike Tyson and Dennis Rodman, all unable to control their actions to fit within a society that demands (or should demand) civility; unable to deal with their desires and ambitions; unable to treat their fellow man with dignity, and instead ignore the people who at one time respected them. And, most recently, we discover the frailty of Tiger Woods, possibly the best Golfer of his generation if not the past 100 years. Like many others, the respect I had for him as a golfer has been soured by his supposedly adulterous actions which eventually precipitated his divorce.

In the New Testament, Romans 12:9-13, we are instructed how to treat others, and, reading between the lines, how to show respect or in reflection, how to gain it as well . . . *"Love must be sincere. Hate what is evil; cling to what is good. Be devoted to one another in brotherly love. Honor one another above yourselves. Never be lacking in zeal, but keep your spiritual fervor, serving the lord. Be joyful in hope, patient in affliction, faithful in prayer. Share with God's people who are in need. Practice hospitality."*

To test the strength of this writing and to bring it home to your heart, simply create a question for each. Would you respect someone who supported nefarious or sinful activities? Could you respect someone who cared more about themselves than others close to them? And would you respect an individual whose underlying motives for their so-called religious fervor was self-promotion, rather than truly serving their God?

Although the answer to each seems clear, in reality we often become confused. Maybe the word "respect" is overused, or possibly the more accurate statement would be, *misused*. Regardless, we have increasingly adulterated its true meaning by casual association to most anything that seems above the ordinary achievement.

At the beginning of the 21st century we have been shaken by some of the financial stalwarts through disclosure of wrong doing. We have seen companies like Enron, Daewoo and Worldcom fall prey to greed and deception by senior management. And we have seen respected companies like the once mighty accounting firm of Arthur Andersen become entangled and mired in dishonesty because some of their own became slaves to money, ego, and power. Where is their respect now? What has become of the heritage of their thousands of hardworking and honest employees and alumni?

I recently crossed paths with the wife of the managing partner (or more correctly, *ex*-managing partner) of what had once been one of the largest accounting firms in the world. They had first been neighbors of ours when our children were barely out of diapers, and I had watched as her husband worked and traveled relentlessly through the years to make a good life for their family. Over time they moved up socially and financially, being rewarded for all of the hard work and sacrifices they had made. I was too embarrassed for her to ask how her husband was doing, thinking it would only open up sores that would be slow to heal. A few days later, I watched the local news covering the sale of the assets of that office, the beautiful furniture, the original pieces of art . . . the same office that had only months earlier employed hundreds of well intentioned, honest, and dedicated personnel like her husband.

How sad that the acts of so few can cast a shadow on the respect deserved by so many.

Athletes, politicians, business leaders, or ordinary citizens of the world - all are susceptible to loss of respect. Because we are humans, we are fallible; prone to temptation, lusting for more of everything, and rarely satisfied with the status quo. And ultimately, these innate traits of the human character drive us to do things we shouldn't.

I like the expression, "gain respect." Associating the words, respect and gain, is probably one of the best pairings of any two words in the English language. Why? Think of all the ways "gain" is used in our everyday vernacular: *gain* weight, *gain* friends, *gain* a position in power, or *gain* riches. In most cases, the word "gain" becomes synonymous with an incremental increase in something (like me gaining a few unnecessary pounds over the past twenty years).

Respect is like that. It is an incremental increase or gain that occurs over a period of time. Respect is not created in a day, although there are times the entertainment or news industry might want you to think that!

Again the confusion!

There is a lot of what I call "artificially created respect" in the world. As an example, the media is often at fault for characterizing people in such a way as to make us feel they should be respected.

They anoint them with glowing adjectives, relate them to material achievements, and enshrine them in physical monuments.

During political elections celebrities are interviewed for their comments as if they were experts on world affairs, economic issues, and other stances taken by candidates . . . as if their opinion carried a more weighted level of credibility than the average person on the street. Sadly I'm afraid many undereducated people actually pay attention to the answers of those celebrities as if they were valuable. I wonder sometimes how many of the stars that have been temporarily "immortalized" in the sidewalks near Graumans Chinese Restaurant in Hollywood, would be considered for immortalization along the streets of Heaven?

Respect is composed of a number of building blocks described with words like integrity, love, faith, empathy, care, selfless, or heroic. It should not be built with adjectives like big, most, finest, and fastest.

Respect should be derived from how or why you did something, rather than what you did.

Do we respect the person or just their achievements?

Can we respect a person's ideas, but not their actions?

We all have a tendency to place the person in the same bottle with their achievements, and call it respect. Think about it for a moment. You and I can have a respect for the position of President of the United States of America. Does that mean we should respect the person holding office as President if they have adulterous relationships? We can admire a football player for breaking a scoring record, but should we respect them when their life is filled with drugs. And can we respect a friend if they continually "entertain" others with racially or ethnically motivated jokes?

Have I done things that have cost me respect? Unfortunately the answer, many times repeated, is "yes".

Sometimes the loss of respect is most quickly reflected in those closest to you . . . particularly in the eyes of children. For them, the world begins pure and in their innocence, they believe those they love can do no wrong. It is with time and repeated disappointments we can be begin to lose their respect. It is this way with most relationships.

In "The Magic of Thinking Big" by David Schwartz, a book devoted to changing your thinking patterns in order to achieve what you want in life, he makes an important point about respect. In the chapter titled "You are what you think you are", he essentially states that in order to have the respect of others you must first respect yourself. Many of his examples are based on physical appearances; the clothes you wear or the way you are groomed. How often do we make a judgment of one's stature in life by the way they appear? The same can be said about respect.

How are we viewed by the rest of the world when they look at our actions, know our attitudes, or observe our adherence to our faith? Do they give us respect or do they try and avoid us. In a way it's a prophetic statement since the word respect is derived from the Latin word *"respect(us)"* meaning to look back as in *"to look back to see something of value - to re spect"*. Will people we know look back some day on us and see something of value?

When we look at ourselves through the eyes of God, what do we see?

Almost 2000 years ago Socrates said, *"The greatest way to live with honor in this world is to be what we pretend to be."* He was absolutely right, because the quickest way to lose respect is to be discovered as being someone different from who you have portrayed yourself to be.

I will never forget as a young teenager, listening to the senior senator from Georgia, Herman Talmadge, speak of what it meant to represent us in Congress.

Although I cared little for politics at that time, I sat only a few feet away in awe of the man, respecting his position and what seemed a sincere interest in helping us as our representative.

Here was a man who had been elected to Congress, eventually serving 24 years, after he had already been Governor of Georgia for 6. Here was a man who after beginning his career supporting policies of segregation was able to change and accept the quality and rights of all human beings regardless of their race. And here was a man that in a later term of office worked to help provide aid to small rural towns to speed industrial development, something that had long been ignored but very much needed to keep the youth from fleeing to the larger cities.

How disillusioned I was just a decade later when I learned he was allegedly filling his own pockets with what was assumed to be misappropriated campaign funds or payoffs from contributors. He was denounced by the Senate, lost re-election in 1980, and twenty-two years later, in early 2002, died at the age of 88 with little fanfare.

In order to overcome the challenge of gaining and keeping respect, we must constantly measure ourselves to a higher standard.

During life we establish the principles by which we live and interact with others. If the principles are sound and honest, then they should be an unchanging guide for us. Unfortunately for some this is not the case.

Groucho Marx, a long-lived American comedian of the 20th century once remarked, *"These are my principles; if you don't like them I have others."* Sadly, many people operate on this premise. To the public audience or a group of colleagues they show one set of their "principles", but in reality, live by a totally different collection.

We must remember the guiding words of our faith. And most of all, we must be able to respect ourselves in all that we do and think. If we can accomplish those things, we will gain the respect of those who know us, and most important, be respectful in the eyes of our God.

Study Guide – Chapter IV
Respectively Yours

Every human wants some level of respect. Even the most hardened criminal would probably want the respect of other criminals. Sadly, that type of perverted form of respect has value to some people. Considering the kind of respect that God would find acceptable answer the following:

1. Read 1Peter 2:18-21. How do you interpret the act of showing respect, even when someone does not act respectable?

2. Make a list of five reasons for which most people would not (or should not) give you respect, (even if people you know are not aware of those reasons). How difficult would it be for you to diminish or eliminate those reasons?

3. What is the most repeated disrespectful thing you do? Is it something you can eliminate on your own, or do you need the help of others?

4. Put together a plan to eliminate your most frequent action that could cause others not to respect you and then solicit the support of God and those close to you in making it vanish - dedicate at least 10 minutes each day to this task. The 10 minutes might include prayer, reading, talking to someone for guidance, writing about the problem, etc.

Group Discussion

1. Pick one male and one female public figure which the majority of the group believe are generally respected, and discuss the reasons why. Some members may want to contradict the view of the majority.

2. During the discussion did any member of the group change their opinion and if so, why?

3. Using the same section of 1 Peter as cited in the first individual discussion point above, discuss the pros and cons of giving respect to those that do not act respectably. Is the writer talking about the position or the actual person?

4. Why does the group think that the Old Testament writings often emphasize the fear of God? Should respect ever be given because of being afraid of pending consequences?

Chapter V

WARM HANDS

Over the past several millennia, many cultures have developed bathing as a ritual. Two of the most famous are the Romans and Japanese. And, although their techniques and approach vary, they all have one thing in common . . . the "baths" were not created primarily for keeping clean!

Today, throughout Europe, are remains of buildings constructed by the Romans to celebrate the art and practice of bathing. Although you may already be familiar with the architectural and engineering feats of the Romans, you may still be amazed at the attention and effort they put into their baths. Bathing was a social event!

Most of the structures relied on a single furnace, external to the actual building, that supplied the heat for not only the water, but for the entire facility. Using the natural draft of numerous small chimneys built around the outside perimeter of the structure, the hot air would be drawn from the furnace, under the tile or marble floors and up through ceramic tubes in the walls, finally joining into one of the chimneys. Heat could be concentrated to specific retaining pools of water where the baths would actually occur. Because of this design, the walls, floors, and water, all could remain warm, even on the coldest of days. Yet today, our modern architects have not seen fit to "catch up" to our ancient brethren.

Although some of the outlying facilities were relatively small, only accommodating a few bathers at one time, many of the structures could easily afford 50 or more individuals the privilege of sharing in the experience simultaneously. And, it was truly an experience!

Often they would spend hours in or around the bath, eating meals, drinking wine, and listening to a musician (one certainly hopes they were neat).

The Japanese too, believe a bath is much more than an act of becoming physically clean. Instead, the "Ofuro" is a daily practice for the majority of Japanese, where on average, they spend a half hour relaxing and meditating in water so hot most westerners would find it intolerable.

For the Romans of two thousand years ago, and the Japanese today, the bath is an escape to a period of reflection, meditation and relaxation brought on by the simplest of elements, *warm water*. Maybe it's because we began life surrounded by the warm water that cushioned our development before birth, or maybe it's because our bodies are composed mostly of water, maintained at a relatively hot temperature as compared to the rest of our living planet. Regardless, our nature is to enjoy and appreciate the surrounding warmth it can bring to us.

I think the same can be said for friendships. There is a warmth that comes to our heart and spirit when we are with a friend. Much like the water, their care, support, and love surrounds us, giving us an opportunity to relax in a way we find impossible with strangers. Friends are able to share in our innermost feelings, soothe our soul when we are in turmoil, and lift our spirits when we are flying low to the ground. They encourage our faith in ourselves and in our God.

Jacques Delille, a French poet who lived from 1738 to 1813 wrote, *"Fate chooses your relations, you choose your friends."* There are stories of friendships that span the generations; stories that can still affect our lives when we read about them. Jesus wisely chose his disciples as friends, and in return they chose him.

How do we measure whether a relation with another person is a true friendship, or whether it is only an interface that is dictated by circumstance or necessity? Are there only the acts of friendship, a superficial smile, and emotions that run skin deep; or is there more . . .?

I have a friend, not necessarily one of my nearest or oldest, who has what I see as a terrible habit of describing every powerful business person *he barely knows*, as a "close friend". It's a rare day when I am with him that he fails to mention some C-level executive as a bosom buddy. Apparently trying to establish a perception of having rich or influential friends is very important to him.

Unfortunately perception often is not reality. Even people whom you truly believe to be friends vanish when they are called on in time of need, or when your popularity or riches disappear.

Take Peter, one of the more outward and vocal disciples of Christ, and a person anyone would have recognized as a friend of Jesus. He was not afraid to express himself, offer criticism, or provide support when needed. Yet, when in the darkest of times, did he stand up and be counted for his God?

In the book of Matthew, 26:33, Peter said to Jesus, *"Even if all fall away on account of you, I never will."* To paraphrase, *"Regardless of what others do, you can count on me Jesus."*

Jesus, as you may know, told Peter that when the chips were down, he would deny any association with him, and predictably Peter responded, *"Even if I have to die with you, I will never disown you."*

Can't you imagine this conversation, and the emotional tone that must have permeated the dinner meeting? And although there are no exclamation points at the end of sentences in the Bible, you can be assured there was definitely the sound of conviction from Peter's voice. Haven't you had "friends" tell you in no uncertain terms, *"If you need me, I'll always be there for you,"* only to somehow not find the time in the entire day to return your phone call when you really needed their help?

It is hard for us to predict the result of such promises, but it is in our nature to believe when someone says they are our friend, they will carry through with the support they pledge. I feel sure Peter felt that way when he contradicted what Jesus knew to be in his future.

Like many of us, Peter's intent was sincere, but his ability to execute his promise was compromised by selfish interests. And as the story unfolds, we see how Peter denied any connection with Jesus, just as Jesus had said would happen. Out of fear, Peter put himself first, and Jesus, his friend and Lord, second.

~

Based on the hundreds of books, poems, lyrics, and sayings written over thousands of years, friendship is obviously a recurring thought in the minds of many of us. Just visit a library or perform a search on the Internet and you may be surprised at the thousands of books and sites dedicated to friendship.

*We need friends, and at the same time
we need to be friends.*

A thought occurred to me many years ago (which as you will quickly see is not very original) as one definition of a true friend. It would be a person who cared enough about me to drop whatever they were doing, and come to my aid if I called on them . . . they would unselfishly put me in front of themselves. A Greek philosopher, Epicurus, beat me to the thought by only twenty three hundred years, *"It is not so much our friends' help that helps us as the confident knowledge that they will help us."* Isn't that the way with our God? Shouldn't we consider God as we do a friend?

Is friendship a more rare commodity today than in years past? Many people I have talked with seem to believe that.

True, as a society today, maybe we are less isolated, are more integrated as a culture, and mix more frequently with people of different demographic or psychographic backgrounds. Yet do we really get to know more of them as friends through this type of exposure?

The mobility of our society, and the activities that crowd the hours of our days, seem to leave little time to develop true friendships. We almost have to pull out our calendars, smart phones, or PDA's (Personal Digital Assistants) and put our friends on a schedule to even talk to them. And all too often, we may limit that communication to a few words transmitted via poorly written text messages. And slowly, almost like the effect of some diseases, we are losing the ability of communication to our relationships, particularly our friends. Even when we make contact, often is has less value because we fail to allocate the time and care to make it meaningful. Through modern technology we may have more volume of communication, but how meaningful is it?

Like any valuable asset, once secured, friendship should be protected, else it can be quickly stolen by the world around us.

How often have you or I called a friend when we had a problem to discuss, or a moment to celebrate? They are there to give us direction, provide the painful truth, and level our path for us.

My longest and closest friend Mike, who has known me since we were nine, has always been there when I needed to talk *and* is a master at seeing through the "fog". I once remember, as a thirteen year-old, wondering out loud why a particular girl (for whom I had what seemed like a perpetual crush) would barely give me the time of day. As I hung head down, with my legs wrapped around the cross-bar of my old backyard swing, the short painful answer came from Mike's mouth, *"You're fat!"* After vehemently contradicting his statement, (and almost getting into a fight), I finally considered his words as I looked into a mirror later that evening. He was right; I WAS fat!

Oscar Wilde said, *"A true friend stabs you in the front."*, or as Proverbs 27:6 states, *"Wounds from a friend can be trusted, but an enemy multiplies kisses."* Has anyone ever said that true friendship was supposed to be just a bed of roses?

Funny how you can look at yourself for months or years and not see the truth. I resolved to change my eating habits immediately and forego (except on rare occasions) the half-dozen Krispy Kreme donuts that I was inclined to wolf down when some high-school band member, or cub scout "pusher" came selling boxes (almost daily as I remember it - and I still love those donuts but use a bit of self-control). The combination of skipping lunch, cutting back on sweets, and growing about eight inches in height took care of the weight problem by the time I was fifteen or so. I wish it were that easy concerning other challenges we face in life.

There is an old song verse that says, *"you have a friend in Jesus"*. We *do* have a friend through our faith in God. We can open the Bible and read how He bore the burden of the sick and poor as well as the rich. We can see how one's status in life had nothing to do with the way He treated those around Him. And we can see the painful truth about ourselves in His statements. But . . . like a *true* friend . . . we can find the warmth and comfort that is there, like the bath water, surrounding us, providing a unique peace to our daily routine.

~

When we are young, our friendship is more open and nat-ural. We offer our first grade classmate the larger of two cookies, or pick them first when at age 10 we are choosing sides for a game of baseball or soccer. We share secrets, make pacts, and create imaginary worlds together. And, we think we are undefeatable!

As we age, our requests to our friends become more com-plex or self-serving. For instance, a teenager will ask a friend to find out if a particular person will go on a date with them (so they don't have to face the embarrassment if that person says "no").

When I attended Georgia Tech, I had a close friend by the name of Terry. He and I were always trying to figure out the opposite sex. (Of course, as I have grown older, I have discovered this is one of those puzzles that has no an-swer). Regardless, we would do most anything to help the other person.

Once I remember spending hours on the phone with one of his ex-high school sweethearts, pretending to be someone else, all the while trying to determine if she still liked him. It seemed all quite normal at the time - why not, he was my friend wasn't he? In retrospect, it now seems like a scene from a poorly scripted "B" movie.

Of course, as we grow older, we do not necessarily grow wiser in how we keep and nurture our friendships.

As careless adults, we can inadvertently begin down the path of potentially abusing our friends. A common example is expecting them to use other relationships as stepping stones to *our* business or social success. Sometimes with little thought, we place them in awkward positions where they must compromise their loyalty to their organization or to other friends in order to satisfy our needs. In a way, we are blackmailing them with our friendship. It is imperative that we do not do this to our friends though they may be willing to help us, even as tempting the circumstances may be.

Don't always think about what they can do for you, but instead think about what you can do for them. In a way, friendship is like gifts at Christmas. It's always better to give than receive!

~

Although I have certainly had my share of baths over the years, they were never in the realm of what the Romans and Japanese have made them. However, many times I have come in from the cold and run warm water over my hands to take the chill away. And as I stand there, I often turn the water even hotter, almost to the point of being unbearable. Yet, there is always this, almost euphoric sensation that traverses my body, decreases my breathing rate, and brings a relaxed feeling to every part of me. I've had similar experiences when meeting friends. It's a good feeling and one I will miss some day when those individuals are no longer in my life.

Did you know that friends are not only good for the spirit, but good for your health?

Medical research has shown that people with a good cadre of friends will live longer than those without - potentially as much as 22% longer.[10] Maybe it's because they look out for you, are there to care for you, or encourage you to stay well. Or, maybe it's simply because the power of their love as felt by you, lifts your mental wellness and that in turn protects you physically. (By the way, being a good friend to several people has the same positive effect on your health). Regardless, the facts speak for themselves.

The lesson here is not only go to the gym, but go be with your friends.

We must be thankful for friendships, challenge ourselves to keep them, and not be afraid to hear the truth or heed their advice. Most important, as the American poet, Ralph Waldo Emerson stated, *"The only reward of virtue is virtue; the only way to have a friend is to be one."*

Every time you warm yourself with a bath or just run hot water over your cold hands, think about the soothing comfort of your friends, and your friendship with God. And, as a friend, know He will be there when you need Him most.

Challenge yourself to be a friend.

Friends can come and go, but if we so choose, some last a lifetime.

Study Guide – Chapter V
Warm Hands

We have opportunities to make and keep friendships all of our lives. It is our responsibility to either keep or lose them. Sometimes physical boundaries make it more difficult when we find ourselves moving to another city, state, or country. However, with the prevalence of multiple channels of communication available today - mail, telephone /cell phone, video, text messages, social Internet sites, email, etc. - most of us have no physical excuse to not maintain friendships once formed. However, there are many other factors that influence whether we make and keep friendships.

1. Are there individuals that were once considered close friends by you but are no longer in your life? Why not?

2. Have you lost a friend through some action of yours that was not acceptable by that person? Was it something you believed was right at that time, and if so, why? Has your opinion changed as you have gotten older (and maybe wiser).

3. Most close friends find it easy to share their innermost feelings with one another. Are you able to do this with your God? Why or why not?

4. Why does sharing your thoughts and emotions with a friend seem like the right thing to do? What do you expect from them when you do this?

5. Are you a "giver" or "taker" relative to your friendships - in other words, do you do more for your friends than they do for you, or it is the reverse? Explain by example.

6. Do you have as many friends as you would like and if not why to you feel that way? Is it something you can change by yourself?

7. If you do want more friends, what are you currently doing about changing the situation, and if you are not taking some action, what type of help would you need? (Now would be a good time to contact a friend and discuss the issue with them - right?)

8. Do you think of God as a friend?

Group Discussion

Given that you are about to discuss this chapter as a group, consider each of the following as if you are all close friends (as you might actually be).

1. Can a friend always be helpful - why or why not?

2. Is it more difficult to ask a group of friends for advice rather than just one friend? Discuss and explain.

3. Do you believe several friends working together can offer more assistance than just seeking support from one friend at a time? Explain.

4. Would Jesus consider all of the Disciples as close friends, just some of them as close friends, or none of them? How is this conclusion supported in the Bible? (one place to look is in the Chapter of John)

Chapter VI

CHOOSE YOUR WEAPON

As a child, there were certain stories in the Bible that seemed more fascinating than others, stirred my imagination, and produced mental images that remain just as vivid today. Probably the one I see most clearly through my mind's eye is that of the destruction of Sodom and Gomorrah.

You may already know the punishment for this most evil and sinful place was the rapid and fiery destruction of the city. It is described in Genesis 19:24, *"Then the Lord rained down burning sulfur . . . (covering over) . . . the entire plain including all those living in the cities and also the vegetation in the land."* Earlier in this story, the main character, "Lot", had been warned to flee with his family away from the city and go to higher ground. The details of the destruction and the safety warning to Lot both lend credence to a naturally occurring phenomenon that scientists call a "pyroclastic flow".

A pyroclastic flow is a combination of ash, soil, and gases that is vented usually from the side of an active or previously dormant volcano. This lethal combination of materials will reach temperatures of several thousand degrees; about the same as the surface of our sun. In addition to spewing outwardly at right angles from its source, like water it will flow downward following the natural lay of the land, approaching speeds of over 100 miles an hour - even crossing stretches of open water. It is easy to understand how any living thing in its path would be destroyed. Obviously, the only way to avoid such a catastrophe would be to find higher ground or increase your distance from the event. Lot and most of his family survived by going as fast as they could to another city, out of harm's way.

The area of the world as described in this Biblical story is still considered seismically active as it was during the time of the early Hebrews. A pyroclastic flow is a natural disaster still to be faced by many of their descendants (and still a potent enforcer at God's disposal).

Although seismologists and volcanologists have tried to accurately predict when such an event will happen, they are more often than not, caught by surprise when one occurs. The only warning to earlier civilizations was the smell of sulfur dioxide, (like rotten eggs) and possibly an increase in the frequency of earthquakes. Pyroclastic flows have occurred frequently around the world, including the 1980 Mt. St. Helen eruption in the state of Washington, the Unzen Volcano eruption in Japan in 1993 and the 2010 Eyjafjallajokull (I can't pronounce it either) volcanic event in Iceland.

We will never know exactly how the two men who came to warn Lot knew of the pending doom, but regardless, they sought out those few who in the eyes of God were worth saving. God's anger destroyed while His love saved.

Anger and love are two emotions that seem about as far apart as black and white, yet they are very often intertwined in our everyday life as they were in the time of Lot. One represents the worst we have to offer while the other, our best.

In the "Old Testament", the writers tell of God's swift and usually harsh punishment of those that sinned. The destruction of Sodom and Gomorrah was certainly a prime example. The "New Testament", in contrast, portrays a God who is more apt to be in concert with the often repeated Hebrew confessional phrase, *"slow to anger and abounding in love"*, found in several books of the Bible from Exodus 34:6 to its last appearance in Jonah 4:2.

I would like to think I follow the latter course of restraint when it comes to losing my temper. "Think" is the key word here, for, in reality (and all too frequently), I am not as patient as I should be.

My first new car was a Ford Mustang. I think I spent more time cleaning and pampering that car than any I have every owned. I was a senior at Gordon High near Atlanta and was proud every time I drove the sunshine yellow "horse" into the school parking lot.

Around Christmas, some of the girls had seasonal jobs at one of the large downtown Atlanta department stores and I committed to carrying them to work. I had already taken a job at one of the banks to pay for the car and so it was not really out of my way, plus a couple of my passengers were cheerleaders, and for a seventeen year-old boy, not bad ridership!

On one particular day, I exited to the right from the expressway with the music blaring and the girls talking. Thinking the boringly white car in front had pulled into traffic, I looked to my left and accelerated right into the back of a police cruiser. The impact against their trailer hitch did no damage to their car, but put a nice dent in the middle of my bumper. The officers made a quick inspection and then headed off to their shift change, apparently not wanting to take the time to give me a ticket. The girls of course got a great laugh out of the incident at my expense and giggled all the way to where I dropped them off.

Before continuing to work, I headed to my father's office, coincidentally across the street from the police station and about four blocks from where I worked at the First National Bank of Atlanta. I thought I could blow off some steam trying to blame the police for not moving into traffic when the way had appeared clear . . . obviously an attempt to off-load my guilt and responsibility.

I went through the entire episode with my father and waited for some comments of agreement. Unfortunately (and rightly so) Dad had no sympathy for what had happened, which made me extremely angry. With him standing on the front loading dock of his business, I hopped in the car, threw it in reverse, revved up the 289 cubic inch Ford engine, released the clutch and inadvertently backed into the quarter panel of his car parked on the other side of the small lot! (He really liked that "slant 6" Dodge).

I need not explain the consequences of that act nor a few choice words he had for me, but it was a justified end to my stupidity. In addition to failing to look in the rearview mirror, this is a prime example of how anger, left uncontrolled, can only cause more damage than good.

Of course I often made other people angry as well including my only sibling, Janet. Making fun of someone six years younger was easy when you are nine years old as I once remember doing; with bad consequences. I don't remember specifically what I did or said, but even at the age of three she found a way to position two of my model planes behind the door of my bedroom such that when she pushed it open quickly, they soon lay in several, unrecoverable pieces. From one aspect, I got what I deserved even though neither events should have happened.

There is tremendous value in those seven words cited earlier - *"slow to anger and abounding in love"*.

The first three, *"slow to anger"* opens a large list of options. It implies having adequate time to contemplate action; being able to develop a measured response to the source of our anger; mustering the resources at our disposal to execute our decision; and finally, placing all events in perspective. I'm afraid most of us begin and end with only the second point: in other words, executing a decision with whatever is most conveniently at our disposal.

~

My father was a "belt man"; my mother, a switch connoisseur. Each implement of punishment dictated the speed at which the anger was released and the subtle nuance of pain such corporal punishment would inflict. Dad had a quick-draw technique with the belt that, unless I was very fast, could catch me across the back of the legs before I could make one good step to run.

Mom, on the other hand, usually sent me to find the switch she would then use on me. Like some golfers I know, she was very discriminating in the flex, diameter, and length of the "device". It had to be just right.

In the early years, there were several times I had to make two or more trips to get a switch that would pass her standards. By the time I was eight or nine, I could easily tell if I had selected the right implement much like a wine expert can discriminate between ten samples of different Chardonnay's. Even then, I might try and pawn-off an inferior selection in order to reduce the pain (very dry and larger diameter was best for that purpose). But most of the time she saw through the ruse and sent me back for a green skinny choice (these by far hurt the most) and added a couple of extra "whacks" for the attempt at deception.

Dad's punishment was scarier, but over in an instant. Unless I had been successful at making a run for it, there was no time to think about what was to happen. Mom's punishment, in contrast, had this nasty psychological aspect to it. Not only did I have more than enough time to think about the pain, but was forced to choose the "executioner's ax" to be used against me.

I can remember crying on the way to the woods to get the switch several times, being very distressed at the anticipation of the forthcoming event. Of course this time-delay gave me other choices, all of which I tried more than once. These included, leaving for the switch and continuing on to a friend's house (this is the "hope she forgets" scenario); developing some lawyerly defense strategy (must have watched too many Perry Mason episodes); or hoping Dad would come home and take my side (only happened once as I remember it).

Corporal punishment seemed to have been more in vogue those days. After W.W.II, Dr. Benjamin Spock became synonymous with the "spare the rod" theory and was influential in the decreased use of physical punishment. One could argue both sides of the approach, but that's a discussion left for another day. Unfortunately, I don't think my parents read his books. That brings us to the last four words of, "*slow to anger, and abounding in love*".

If, and that's a BIG "IF", we eventually become angry and feel inclined to deal out punishment, then we should do so in the right *frame of heart*.

The challenge God lay's before us is one of the most difficult we can face. Can we let our emotion of love, temper our anger and block other punitive actions based on feelings as hate, malice, envy, and fear?

Do we have enough of God's wisdom to act wisely?

When fighting a battle, most military commanders have numerous weapons at their disposal. Depending on the specific engagement, tactics may call for close combat infantry, long range shelling of targets, use of quick-strike air-mobile units, laser guided missiles or fighter aircraft. Smart commanders usually work on what one might call a plan of "minimization". Expressed another way, the intent of a battle is to minimize expenditure of armaments; minimize civilian casualties; minimize the time to execute the plan; minimize loss of life; and minimize collateral damage. Essentially it is to execute a plan that is effective and efficient.

In contrast, the military vernacular for overuse of resources of any kind (which has crept into our everyday vocabulary) is the word "overkill". Thus, choosing the right weapons is a very important part of their strategy. So too is how we deal with anger.

Too often we become angry and then fail to follow a plan of minimization.

We may physically strike out such as hitting our children, or sometimes worse, fire a salvo of cruel words that hurt well beyond the whelps a spanking might leave. We often overreact and "overkill". And we often do it to everyone around us. Ephesians 4:26 states, *"In your anger do not sin."*

Anger can cause not only over-reaction, but a loss of control; mentally and even physically. How often has a convicted felon stated, *"I didn't mean to kill the person."* And, maybe they didn't. But, potentially their anger and inability to control their action precipitated by that feeling, did result in someone's death . . . a sin that will forever be blazoned on their soul.

How often do we react in anger to a minor annoyance?

Stop and consider the number of people who are shot or shot at each year because they accidentally or intentionally squeezed too close in front of another driver who then lost control of their emotions. Are there weapons that are non-destructive that can be used instead to resolve conflicts? The military thinks so.

Current research into such weapons has been underway for many years. Prototypes are being tested that can temporarily incapacitate groups of individuals through a reasonably loud unidirectional burst of high-pitched sound, with no permanent damage to their hearing. Another potential weapon is an oily substance that is so slippery, that when sprayed over troops and lightweight vehicles, they are unable to move, almost as if they were on ice.[11]

What if we as parents, teachers, friends, or even strangers chose non-destructive weapons to use? Can we be smart enough and patient enough to eliminate the source of our anger without destroying it? Yes, I've angrily made a gesture at a careless driver, but I've also laughed when another person committing the same offense waved at me after realizing their mistake. Maybe I should always laugh or smile at those kind of situations, even if the other driver does not wave!

In Matthew, 5:39 Jesus said, *"If someone strikes you on the right cheek, turn to him the other also."* This mollified the prevailing practice (and one which continues today in some parts of the world) of an *"Eye for eye, and tooth for tooth,"* Mat. 5:38. In other words, if I take your life, my life is expected to be taken.

Jesus practiced and taught forgiveness. Even as he died on the cross, with enemies all around, Jesus forgave those who were killing him. He could have cursed these people from his anger, but he didn't. Think about that.

An old adage says that when you are angered and about to do something (you may regret), first stop and count to 10.

I would modify that and say "*stop and count your bless-ings*".

If you child does something that irritates you, be thankful you have children. If your wife overcooks a steak you were looking forward to, be happy she was there for you. And if a friend forgets to thank you for that free ticket to the ball game you gave him, just count him as a blessing because he is your friend.

~

Many people may not know that Abraham Lincoln, consid-ered one of the most important presidents of the United States, put his life in jeopardy by making someone angry through his words. During his early life he had a habit of criticizing anyone with whom he disagreed. Not only did he vocalize his criticism, he often wrote and published his destructive words. One such person became so angered, he challenged Lincoln to a duel. Although not inclined to physical violence, Lincoln reluctantly agreed.

According to the rules, the opponent got to choose the weapons. Although guns were the rule of the day, Lincoln chose broad swords. Why? Because of his height, his arms were exceptionally long with an estimated reach 6 - 8 inches over most men. He judged that in swinging a sword he should be able to contact his foe before he could be struck himself.

Luckily, we will never know what the outcome would have been because the duel was stopped moments before it was to start. But at least it appears Lincoln had a good strat-egy regarding his choice of a weapon, crude that is was. Unlike Lincoln, when dealing with other people *our weapon does not have to be physical or destructive.*

In the 1981 best-selling book "*The One Minute Manager*", by Kenneth Blanchard and Spencer Johnson, they state that in order to motivate someone in the direction you want them to go such as in reaching their full potential, *"catch them doing something right"*. Positive motivation is a great weapon. Instead of becoming angry and critical, select a strategy that rewards a behavior that does not anger you . . . even if that behavior is self-directed! Make it work with everyone around you and when you fail as I often do, get up, dust your anger off, and try again. Throw away your list of negative words and replace them with words of encouragement.

Forget about power plays, egos, and damaged feelings, and instead, wield a weapon of forgiveness, compassion, understanding, and love.

Are there times to become angry? Absolutely! Should we punish others through our anger? Absolutely not!

Not too long ago I attended a sermon by Andy Stanley, who as the son of the noted minister, Charles Stanley, wears similar "shoes" but is walking in them down a slightly different path to the same goal. In his very casual way one Sunday morning he related a story about himself. Often he would come home from work and find his garage so overrun by toys that he could not pull his car into the space and park.

He would get out, move the offending items out of the way, park the car, and then being mad, go and lecture his kids about why they should keep the garage clean. This would work for a few days, but eventually things would return to "normal".

One day he pulled up to the garage and saw the toys blocking his path. But this time his eyes saw a different picture and he gained an entirely new perspective. To paraphrase, *"How many people would give their right hand if they could pull up and see children's toys scattered in front of them?"*

How often do we take for granted what we have, or fail to appreciate the life God has given us? Are we slowly destroying those around us with anger or are we gently guiding them with a superficially painful nudge?

There is an often repeated phrase in movies when a parent is spanking a child which goes *"this is going to hurt me a lot more than it will hurt you."* When the time comes (and it will) for you to spank, criticize, or levy punishment, make sure that previous statement is always true!

In researching the word, *weapon*, I was surprised it directly followed two other words in both of my dictionaries - "wealth" and "wean". Wouldn't we be *wealthier* individuals if we could *wean* ourselves from weapons of destruction and select a course of action that places everyone out of harms way? And wouldn't our souls be at more peace if we could abide by the last part of Ephesians 4:26, *"Do not let the sun go down while you are still angry,"*. Not only would we be better for obeying that recommendation, but probably those around us would appreciate the effort as well.

Following those seven words, *"slow to anger, and abounding in love"*, how can we go wrong?

Study Guide – Chapter VI –
Choose Your Weapon

We are often put in the position of having to initiate corrective action to remedy a situation. It could take the form of parents trying to reel in an overly exuberant child; of a teacher attempting to improve a student's work; a policeman trying to stop a speeding car; or the military combating a rogue nation. Regardless, we usually have a choice of "weapons" we can employ to solve the problem at hand.

Carefully consider each of the following as you think about what "weapon" is best for the situation or if the course of action is appropriate:

1. If you saw a man in the middle of a grocery isle insulting his wife for picking the wrong type of cereal and then loudly calling her names, how would you feel if he then looked at you when he noticed your presence? Would you say something to alleviate the situation? Why or why not?

2. Can you think of an instance when you only delivered negative criticism to a spouse or friend that resulted in a positive change? If so, what was the initial situation and outcome? Do you feel it was justified? In retrospect was it the best approach?

3. List 5 negative words or phrases that you might find yourself using to criticize someone or some object. Then list five alternatives that sound more positive. (ex. "You must be stupid if you don't understand those directions." as compared to "It seems I may not have given you very good directions.")

Group Discussion

1. Does corporal punishment have a place in modern society? Why or why not?

2. When arguments result in front of children or in public, what type of "collateral damage" often results? Give specific examples.

3. Why do you believe that God is represented in the New Testament as a much more understanding and benevolent entity as compared to the Old Testament?

4. In dealing with either children or subordinates in business, which do you believe has more of a direct effect on motivation; fear, respect, or both? Explain each opinion expressed in the group.

5. Should God be feared by mankind?

Chapter VII

IN PERSPECTIVE

Where do you stand in God's universe? It's a simple question with what seem very complex answers.

In 1990, the Hubble space telescope was launched, and, after a few repairs and technical improvements through the years, has become what some believe to be the most valuable instrument to our understanding of the universe ever created. With the various imaging devices which allow the viewing of both visible light, and also electromagnetic radiation in spectrums humans cannot see, scientists have looked hundreds of times further into space than ever before, and back in time as well.

What they have found seems almost incredible! There are gaseous clouds millions of miles across giving "birth" to new stars. In several locations, hot streams of plasma (superheated electrons), shoot from the center of a star, focused into a beam by strong invisible magnetic forces much like a glass lens focuses light. And, after years of speculation, there has been visible confirmation that other stars have planets, much like our own solar system.

More recently, just a few years ago, scientists focused the Hubble telescope on a very small area of space in order to determine the extent of other galaxies in the universe. To give you an idea of the size of space that was surveyed, take a ¼ inch square piece of paper and hold it against the night sky at arm's length. That will give you a fair estimate of the quantity of space they viewed - *not very much.*

In that one very, very small area, they counted almost 2000 galaxies! As you may already know, our galaxy, called the "Milky Way" has an estimated 150 *billion* stars, our Sun being one of them. Our's is a good, middle-of-the-road representative. So if we multiply those almost 2000 galaxies by 150 billion stars and then factor in all of the rest of space still left to survey, we come up with an estimated number of stars that would have 26 zeros after the 1

(100,000,000,000,000,000,000,000,000)

Some scientists speculate, on average, at least one planet for every star exists; some habitable and many that are not.[12]

It is unlikely that our generation, or even the next several, will ever know if life as we understand it exists elsewhere, but the probability is very high that we are not unique in this respect.

Unfortunately we are still infants in the technologies it will take to allow us to explore other solar systems within our own galaxy, yet alone traveling to other whirling masses of stars millions of light years from here. What we are certain of is that relative to this universe, earth appears as but one very, very, VERY tiny spec. Even on our own planet, you or I are one of over 6.2 billion humans. So . . . given all these statistics . . . does it make you feel insignificant?

Every day we are not only challenged to be significant, but more importantly, every hour and every minute we are given the opportunity by our God to be a contributing part of this universe. To quote William Shakespeare, " . . . *to be, or not to be, that is the question . . .* "

Some of us worry so much about our significance, we accomplish nothing of significance.

Others feel so insignificant or useless that they end their lives, figuratively, or worse, literally! And others just don't think about it at all, semiconsciously plodding through life day-after-day.

Sadly, in the last year of the twentieth century, over 3 million children in the US between the ages of 12 and 17 considered suicide and approximately one third of those attempted it.[13] The number one reason given was, *they had nothing to live for!*

Albert Camus, a French philosopher and author wrote about the significance of life in a book titled, "The Myth of Sisyphus". As some may know, the mythological story of Sisyphus is one of punishment. It involves the sentence of Sisyphus to forever rolling a rock to the top of a hill at the edge of the living world and then watching it roll back down to the underworld from where he must go and eternally roll it back up again. Camus interpreted this as man's typical routine existence, doing repetitive tasks of work in what he called an absurd world, yet finding periodic happiness in accomplishing nothing of significance.

Maybe that is the way with most people including many Christians and others who profess their religious conviction. They are content with their rituals and pilgrimage to places of kindred spirits, yet outside of this they make no outstanding contribution to their faith. *"Unfortunately,"* as I once commented to someone, *"we often worship as a mob, not as individuals."*

In our hearts, you and I know it is easier to be part of a group than act alone.

As late as the twentieth century, lynch mobs committed terrible crimes that most individuals would never do by themselves. In recent years, using various excuses, gangs of young adults have looted and burned stores, where any one of them would have been unlikely to do such a thing if left to their own devise. And "mobs" of parishioners have exiled members of their congregations because no one individual was able to deal with dissension, or contradictory opinion.

A mob is faceless; it has no name.
A mob is thoughtless; it has no mind.
A mob is guiltless; it has no soul.

Do you want to be part of a mob or be the individual you are born to be?

Paul, writing in Galatians 6:4 states, *"Each one should test his own actions. Then he can take pride in himself, without comparing himself to somebody else, for each one should carry his own load."*

Jesus knew his role in life and he knew it would stand apart from the crowd. In Luke 4:43, after being questioned about why he needed to be moving on after a local visit, he replied to the people, *"I must preach the good news of the kingdom of God to the other towns also, because that is why I was sent."*

God has given man the ability to witness in His name, yet how few are the times we do it, *if ever.*

Do you have to stand on a street corner and shout out your beliefs? Of course not. But through your acts and thoughts you can always silently witness to everyone around you even when you have trouble doing it verbally.

Think of the impact you can have on another person, or on thousands of people. Just consider how Jesus has impacted the life of millions. You might ask, *"how could I possibly influence hundreds or thousands of people?"*

Since I previously used mathematical computations of galaxies, stars, and planets to point to our physical insignificance in the universe, let's do some other calculations to look at our truly amazing opportunity to be significant.

In practicality, our level of significance is directly related to our reach or *realm of influence*. In other words, if there were only one of us on the planet Earth, then our significance would be measured by only our thoughts, and that of God. Our realm would extend only to ourselves. Luckily, we do not face that situation. So what is our realm of influence?

Let's begin by forgetting about mass media and technical crutches such as the Internet as vehicles for expanding our reach. Instead, let's start with a person-to-person calculation. This was the way Jesus influenced his followers . . . the way Abraham communicated to the children of Israel . . . the way other ancient leaders led. Have you ever heard about the six degrees of separation?

Like most people, you and I probably know at least 10 people that do not know each other. And it can be assumed that each of those know 10 more people that are not connected in any shape or form. What if we could give our 10 people a message that we wanted relayed to each of the 10 folks they know, and ask that they continue this for 4 more levels of contact; a total of 6. Mathematically that comes to 10 times 10 times 10 times 10 times 10 times 10, (10^6) or a grand total of one million people! By the way, if you think that number is large, most people actually know somewhere between 25 and 100 unconnected individuals. Just taking the number 25 and going through the 6 levels it would total the approximate population of the United States . . . about 250 million! Using the number 50, we would exceed the population of the earth.

The theory behind "the six degrees of separation" is based on this same mathematical model with one exception. It assumes we influence the direction in which the connections travel. In other words, if we wanted to influence or communicate with a particular person or group anywhere in the world, we could do it by looking for one of our contacts that had a connection in the direction we wanted to go.

As an example, if one of my friends asked me if I knew someone who ran a timber company in Brazil, I would say no, but . . . I did know the president of Georgia Pacific Corporation (we co-managed a group of Boy Scouts in our younger years). I would guess he had a manager who was responsible for South America and that person in turn probably had a connection that knows of a timber company in Brazil. In this example, there are only 3 or 4 degrees of separation between my acquaintance and a representative of a Brazilian timber company.

In theory, there are at most, only 6 degrees of separation between you and any other person in the world. We're a lot more connected than you probably thought. Good salespeople and politicians follow this model do they not? And with the mass media, or the internet, multiple degrees of separation can be overcome in minutes or hours. One public Internet site makes heavy use of this.
www.linkedin.com is used mostly by business people to establish links to others who in turn may provide a link to someone else who in turn may provide a link to . . . well, you get the picture. Today we can "Twitter", post comments on FaceBook, and "blog" to our heart's content. All are ways to communicate our ideas, concerns, or (unfortunately) just useless and ephemeral information.

If we can have a life of significance, just think of the potential realm of influence we have at our disposal.

If we write an inspirational poem and send it to our friends, consider how many it could ultimately inspire. How often will an observed act of kindness be multiplied as a story through its retelling? Will a courteous smile and sincere *"good morning"* be passed on through multiple degrees of separation in one day? On a smaller scale, can performing *only one* significant act have value in this vast universe? Absolutely!

Think of the story of the Good Samaritan beginning in Luke 10:25. The Jews looked down on Samaritans with contempt, considering them as foreigners and half-breeds. Although open hostility existed between the two groups, this particular Samaritan stopped and treated the robbed and beaten Levite as a brother and friend. This example of kindness did not go unnoticed, particularly after Jesus related the story to his disciples as a lesson in how we should treat others.

~

What have I done significantly in my life? Like most, I sometimes think very little. Yet there are those occasions that remind me that maybe I *can* do acts of significance . . . I *can* make a difference.

A couple of years ago while entering a grocery store, I passed a young woman who looked very familiar. We continued on our way, but a few minutes later, she returned and found me in one of the aisles. *"Hi, my name is Shannon"* she said. *"You may not remember me, but I worked for you about 15 years ago and I just wanted to thank you."*

When she said her name, I was able to put her in perspective, but before I could say but a couple of words she continued. *"I have often wanted to tell you of my appreciation because you had enough faith in me to let me get into a sales role, even though no one else believed I could do it. After I left the company, I joined another organization"* (one which I recognized as a pre-eminent player at that time),*" and I became their number one salesperson. If it had not been for you, I would probably have never made it into sales, so thank you."*

She will probably never know how much I appreciated her *"thank you"* but it made me feel very significant that day and for weeks that followed. Obviously it continues to be important to me because here it is in the book.

~

For several years, every Thursday, like clockwork, I received an email from a friend I met through a men's Christian fellowship organization called Leadership Ministries. Weekly, he composed a list of thought provoking or inspirational quotations and distributed it to what I presume was a large list of recipients. I always seemed to find a line or two that struck home with me and lifted my spirit. In turn, I sometimes forwarded these to other friends, extending Bob Varga's realm of influence in the process. Bob was being a significant player in my universe.

Leadership Ministries was founded by another significant individual, Chris White, who, proactively, day-after-day, seeks to make a difference in hundreds of men's lives. Giving up a senior-level sales position for IBM, (a "top gun" in Manhattan), twenty-plus years ago he decided there was better things in life than just a big house, an inflated ego, and the cut-throat office politics that often go with the job. Because of his devotion and focused actions, he has grown the organization to be not only an influencing agent in men's lives in Atlanta, but has organically spread his good work to other parts of the world.

When Vince Lombardy, a great coach, motivator, and inspiration of the Green Bay Packers football team died in 1971, the team figurative died as well. It was many years before they started to achieve even a modicum of the greatness they had obtained under Lombardy's leadership. His unique style, caring, and independence produced those outstanding teams. His influence was a significant factor in his team's lives.

The problem most of us have is accepting the challenge of making a difference. We all have it in us, but we fail to stand apart from the mob.

We let the world overwhelm and bury us with normalcy. And, we allow our doubts to govern us into obscurity.

My favorite cartoon artist is the "pre-maturely retired" Gary Larsen. He often uses animals as a vehicle for poking fun at the human species. One drawing, which I think is appropriate, is a depiction of a group of sheep mostly grazing head down with the exception of a few turning to look at one lonely member of the flock standing up and yelling *"We all don't have to be sheep do we?"*

In God's universe, we *don't* all have to be sheep. We are more than just a spec in the vastness of space. Our lives have value and meaning and you and I know there are more Samaritans among us. We *can* be important to others, and through our realm of influence, guide them toward a better life.

Increase your effectiveness by concentrating time to those issues that matter most rather than waste resources on menial tasks of little value.

Take God's challenge to be significant today and tomorrow, however small or great the opportunity, we can do it if we try. *"To be, or not to be,"* that *is* really the challenge isn't it?

Study Guide – Chapter VII
In Perspective

As you think about all of the tasks being faced each day, and how you allocate your time, consider the following:

1. When is the last time you intentionally did something that positively affected another person or group? What motivated you to do it? How long did it take?

2. Is there someone in your life that you feel compelled to help spiritually? If you answer "yes", then why? If you answer "no", then why not?

3. Make a list of those tasks you expect to tackle tomorrow and then rank them by importance. Next write the estimated time to complete each one. Beginning from the least important, select and eliminate or postpone as many as necessary to total a minimum of 30 minutes. Finally, consider how you can use that time for something of significance that will affect another person, and then do it!

4. When was the last time you played the role of the good Samaritan? Have you passed by such opportunities because you considered your time to be used more valuably doing something else? Were you being honest with yourself when you made that decision?

5. Would you agree with the statement, "Giving of your time and energy should be done without a promise of getting something in return."? If you answered "yes", then in what way have you succeeded in doing this?

Group Discussion

1. Have each person in the group answer question "5" above and discuss openly.

2. Can a group be more significant in spreading the word of God than its individual members? Discuss taking into consideration the influence of Jesus as compared to the Disciples.

3. Have each member cite one person that had a positive influence on their life and have them describe both direct and indirect effects.

4. Discuss if it is appropriate for the group to identify some act (project, visitation, outreach program, charity, etc.) that could be supported directly by the members and be a positive influencing factor that would last beyond at least one year.

Chapter VIII

HOW ARE YOU MEASURED?

If you asked most people who was John Paul Jones, they could respond in several ways, but mostly they would say he was an early American hero; the father of the Navy. Others might remember his words as he battled a much larger British warship when he uttered, *"I have not yet begun to fight!"* in response to a request by the commander of the enemy ship to surrender. (Jones eventually won the battle). Would anyone tell you how much he was worth, or how tall he was? There was so much more to his life than most of us could relate.

You may not know that as a Lieutenant he not only commanded the first colonial ship to attack the British, but later he also commanded a combined armada of colonial and French ships during several battles. He loved ships and travel, having started work on a merchant vessel at the age of thirteen. In fact, during his short, forty-five years of life, he was a commissioned officer of the United States, France, and Russia at one period or another.

His last battle was fought for Catherine the Great of Russia, where he was greatly admired by the nobility, but disliked by fellow Russian officers because he was a foreigner. Yet given all that he did, and the admiration we as Americans have bestowed on him, rarely if ever do we think of the fact that he came from humble beginnings as the son of a gardener.

Like many wanderers of his time, he had brushes with the law (even changing his name from John Paul to John Paul

Jones in order not to be found), and although never married, he was more than a "ladies man" having taken many lovers over the years. He was also prone to self-aggrandizement, writing many letters and exaggerated journals detailing his exploits, purportedly to increase his chances of higher ranks for the naval groups he commanded. Others believed the "stretched" truths came from an inferiority complex because of his shorter height (about 5'5" by some estimates).

During Jones' life he accumulated little wealth and died reasonably poor being buried in a rather nondescript grave in France. It was not until early in the twentieth century, in 1913, that his remains were moved to their present resting-place at the US Naval Academy Chapel in Annapolis, Maryland.

How do we measure the value of a person? Is it through their possessions and wealth? Certainly that was not the case with John Paul Jones. Yet how often do we begin describing someone we know in terms of what they have? *"There goes Bill Roseglass. That's him over there in the new Mercedes convertible. Ya know, he made a killing when he invested in that real estate south of the Big Lake Mall."* I know I have found myself prone to do that on more than one occasion.

Even during the time of Jesus, attributes like honor and wisdom were unfortunately equated to what today we would call the person's tangible net worth. The account of King Solomon was a story of power, of a lust for gold, of squandering riches on monuments and palaces, and of the problems when we place our faith in material possessions.

In the book of Ecclesiastes which some attribute to Solomon, it states in 4:4, *"And I saw that all labor and all achievement spring from man's envy of his neighbor. This too is meaningless, a chasing after the wind."*

Regardless of the authorship, it is a sincere statement of one person's reflection on life and how we often toil to gain recognition and riches which ultimately have little meaning. We envy the new car our friend drives, wish our clothes were more in vogue, or forgo our morals to gain political position. Solomon's preoccupation with materialism and power rather than to follow God's commandments led to his demise.

In the chapter "A Precious Loss", I write about attachments and how we form many levels of relationships to both the living and the inanimate. If we rank all that we are attached to, where does faith fit on that scale? Surely faith should be in the first position. If we lost all of the other items that we have on that list, shouldn't faith be the one we want to hold on to until the very end?

In America, our society tends to emphasize "things" over people. How can we ever have greater attachment to something that is inanimate than someone who is flesh and blood?

Although the answer should seem obvious, think how many marriages end because of arguments and financial anguish over one or the other's, seemingly insatiable appetite to accumulate an ever-increasing amount of assets . . . . usually accompanied by a proportionally large burden of debt and worry? Problems created by cars that are too extravagant; houses that are too big (with rooms that are rarely visited); memberships to the best clubs; tuition for the most private of schools.

Are we sacrificing more important relations we could have by attaching ourselves to other "things" that in the end would be of little consequence?

> *When we die, will we not be remembered by what influence we had on others, rather than what material assets we amassed?*

When we act as children of God, doing what He instructs us to do, we will create value far greater than all the gold and silver on earth! From my perspective, I would much rather be remembered like John Paul Jones for the good he accomplished rather than dwelling on the fact that he never had a big house or died poor.

Can my children and wife think of the good times we had talking to one another, or playing some silly game, and in the process not worry about whether we are "keeping up" with the Jones family down the street? Those kind of moments will certainly be more important and bring greater joy than looking at an expensive watch on your wrist. If it's time you're after, a twenty-five dollar timepiece works just as well as a three thousand dollar Swiss movement.

In John Steinbach's gripping novel, *"The Grapes of Wrath"*, we are immersed into the depth of what it was like to lose most everything you physically owned. He writes about the families whose farms were devastated by the "dust bowl" droughts that swept the Midwest and Southwest United States during the 1930's. For those that had deep pockets of money, it was a time of bargains as hundreds of small farms were bought for pennies on the dollar for back taxes, or delinquent bank notes.

One of Steinbach's characters makes the astute observation in chapter 5, *"If a man owns a little property, that property is him, it's part of him . . . and in some way he's bigger because he owns it."* But in contrasting the small farmer to the new land barons he continues, *"But let a man get property he doesn't see, or can't take time to get his fingers in, or can't be there to walk on it - why, then . . . he is small, not big. Only his possessions are big - and he's the servant of his property."*

Who do you know is a better person based on the *quantity* of what he owns?

I have a friend whose path I seem to cross every few years. As kids we competed with each other from rock throwing to seeing who could make the best score in school and, as we grew older, he seemed to beat me on many counts (particularly the scores). He worked very hard in college and achieved his goal of becoming a reasonably wealthy doctor (at a very early age).

There were many times I openly expressed envy at what he had, enjoying the opportunity to take the controls of one of his planes or ride in a car costing three times the price of mine. Luckily, as only a spouse can do, my wife was always there to bring me back to reality.

Unfortunately, like so many meteoric displays in the night's sky, his planes and house and expensive cars all disappeared in a flash when he became over-extended trying to expand his wealth even more. For him, he suffered what some consider the ultimate financial embarrassment - bankruptcy. Even now, several decades later, I believe he has not fully recovered from that period. I often wonder how his life would have been if material possessions had not seemed to be of so much importance to him early in his career.

Some businesses have part of their value stated in terms of what is called "intangible assets". These are items of value you cannot see or touch, but they are real. Think of the value of the name "McDonald's", or "Coca Cola". We too can have intangible values far more important than ones we can sit in or sleep on . . . things like wisdom, kindness, loving, empathy and reputation.

I ran across an interesting government statistic. In 1994, on average, 15.4 percent of Americans were poor each month, and about 22 percent — or 55 million people — were poor for at least two months during that year.[14]

First, it is obvious that many people went through a revolving door of poverty . . . some lasting inside its walls for a very short period, while others stayed much longer. However, what I also found interesting is that research has shown most people we classify statistically as being below the poverty line, don't think of themselves as being poor! It seems that the method our governments use to determine poverty only considers a monetary scale. Yet as people, we often believe we are doing better because we don't measure the quality of life in tangible assets or dollars, but rather by how we feel and what kind of "job" we are doing. In other words, are we a good neighbor, a good parent, or a good and faithful servant of God.

When my wife Ellie and I were first married, some of our best times were spent in our little apartment. She covered cheap snap-together hardboard tables with cloth to disguise them, and did a wonderful job arranging the few pieces of real furniture we had borrowed. And both of us will never forget me rebuilding the engine of an old Volkswagen "Beetle" on the kitchen floor (I don't think she will ever forget me getting motor oil on the curtains she made that covered the sliding-glass door). It was definitely one of several periods where we seemed to live from paycheck to paycheck, but on the scale of happiness, most of the time we were right at the top.

We need to be sure the scales by which we assess ourselves and others are both accurate and relative. Just as we would not use the Kelvin or Centigrade scales to measure the weight of groceries, we should not use the value of accumulated assets to measure happiness.

Look around you. Do you measure the teacher by the car they drive or Mother Teresa by the label in the clothes she wore? Proverb: 20:15: *"There is gold, and a multitude of rubies: but the lips of knowledge are a precious jewel."*

Like so many other innate gifts of God, the ones of most importance are given to us freely and have no economically quantifiable value.

Obviously there is nothing wrong with being wealthy as long as what motivates you is not greed. It should be a by-product of what you are able to accomplish out of the good you or your organization gives to people. If you make a better mousetrap, why should you not be rewarded with more sales? If you are a great artist, why should your paintings not sell for a higher price?

In the end what matters is more than riches. As the inspired writer of Psalm's 49:16-20 penned, *"Do not be overawed when a man grows rich, when the splendor of his house increases; for he will take nothing with him when he dies, his splendor will not descend with him Though while he lived he counted himself blessed - and men praise you when you prosper - he will join the generation of his fathers, who will never see the light of life. A man who has riches without understanding is like the beasts that perish."*

But what happens if you lose all of those assets you have accumulated? Can you survive without them?

Will others recognize you for who you are rather than what you have? Can you start over once, twice, or be gracious in your material loss, because in the end, what will your world remember about you. Will they say, *"There goes Bill Roseglass. What a great husband and father he has been. He was one of the most forgiving and cheerful people*

I've known, and it's reflected in each of his children and the eyes of his friends."?

One of my favorite poems is by Rudyard Kipling and is called "IF". Although the poem is a message to a child as instructions on how to be a man, we can all learn from its words. This particular set of edited verses seems more than appropriate:

" If you . . .(can) . . . watch the things you gave your life to broken, and stoop and build them up with worn-out tools,

. . . and lose and start again at your beginnings and never breathe a word about your loss, . . .

Yours is the Earth and everything that's in it, and which is more, you'll be a man, my son."

I'm not much of a risk taker unless you consider racing motocross or flying small planes in that category. I've certainly had my share of bad investments, lost property, or made dumb purchases. So, it is difficult for me to describe the feeling of having to risk everything only to lose and have to start over. But stories like *The Grapes of Wrath*, can make me more clearly understand the emotional and spiritual challenges one would face.

Similarly, I have never known what it would be like to be really poor . . . unable to put food on the table for your family, or buy clothing to keep you warm. But I have seen it in several countries where I've traveled.

One vivid memory is of two beautiful children, definitely decendents of the Incas, standing near the front of the vehicle in which I was traveling. They stood begging for food in a little village several hours outside of Bogota, Columbia not far from a cathedral carved into an old salt mine. Although their native clothing was worn through in spots, they were neatly dressed, and held themselves with dignity. And like most children, you could see the sparkle in their eyes, as they looked up the steps into our bus. They were still young enough not to fully appreciate the economic conditions in which they lived.

I'm sure at some time in their future they became aware of the vast differences between their world and the hustle of Bogota, a city of over 10 million people just a few hours away. Would they lose part of that vitality that made their faces light-up when someone smiled at them . . . lost because of being measured against what they did not have in ways of material assets? Would their smiles turn into the sullen and hardened stares of their parents?

~

Television ads and movies often show us what we don't have in a planned effort to make us want more of what they are offering. They want us to feel possession "impoverished". It's too bad they don't show more of us how we are spiritually impoverished. Wouldn't that be great? I'm reminded of what an advertising executive once told me. *"The public needs this product . . . they just don't know it yet!"*

Vance Packard wrote a book several decades ago titled *"Hidden Persuaders"*. It describes many ways we as consumers are inundated by companies to entice us to make purchases. Some tactics border on the unethical. Often they prey on the undereducated, impoverished, or aged. Like his descriptions in the book, we must be on guard to not be influenced by all types of temptations to take what we have. *Our* hidden persuaders may come not in just the form of well crafted advertisements, but from pseudo-friendships, indirect relationships, and even the leadership in organizations where we work or worship.

In the first decade of the 21st Century, America lost it's business sense when it allowed monetary goals of investment bankers and others to provide loans (particularly mortgages) to people who could least afford them. Instead of helping the borrowers become long- term home owners, their greed ultimately crippled not only the individuals but the country. Yet, these people were both directly and indirectly persuaded that home ownership was the right thing to do without being warned about the consequences if the economy turned sour . . . which it did.

~

God's challenge to us is to realize that *we can never lose what is in us* and not let all that is around us keep us from our faith, regardless of the material temptations of our world or the monetary losses we might suffer.

Your faith is yours, and yours alone, and no one can ever take it from you. But if you're not careful, other "things" of temporal value can make you forget it's there.

How will you be measured by those you leave behind? In what way will you invest while you live? What will be your brand equity? What intangible assets of your life will those you encounter be left when you are no longer on this earth?

It's up to you and God.

Study Guide – Chapter VIII
How are you measured?

Over the centuries humans have developed all types of measuring devices and scales. Some have worked very well and lasted over time while others have lost their significance. Many are named after the people who developed them (the Kelvin or Fahrenheit scales for temperature), while others are derived from some physical aspect of the scale ("hands" for measuring a horse's height, or "foot" for linear measurements, being the approximate length of a Mediaeval person's foot).

As you read each question or point of discussion below, consider which types of systems and scales are valuable in measuring our lives.

1. Write down a list of at least 10 dimensional ways to measure yourself. Then remove all of those that apply to only physically tangible traits (height, weight, etc.) and create a scale for each that remain. Rank yourself on each scale and consider if that position is where you want it to be (low/high, a-b-c, etc.). If you are not satisfied with any ranking, make a plan to improve your position on that scale and then re-measure yourself every 90 days to check your progress.

2. Is it important to you to be ranked higher than those around you? If so, why? Did Jesus care about ranking?

3. Write your own epitaph such that if you were to die today, you would like to have it read at your funeral. Put it away for a couple of days, review it and then rewrite it if necessary. Did you make any significant changes and if so why?

4. Ask three friends to write your epitaph using less than 100 words and see what they say. Is it what you expected and if not, why?

5. Ask your spouse or children to write your epitaph. Again, is it what you expected or wanted them to say?

Group Discussion

1. Ask every person in the group to write down each person's name and then beside it, place only one word that they believe best describes that person. Then, taking one individual at a time, have each member read the word they chose for that person and then briefly explain why they selected that word. See if there are general trends or wide differences and discuss why they may exist.

2. In what terms did Jesus measure others? Support your premises with references to specific verses in the Bible.

3. Discuss how different cultures may measure personal achievement. Cite specific examples.

4. Ask for volunteers to describe what types of measurable results the organizations to which they belong look to achieve. This can include their place of employment. Openly discuss the pros and cons of each.

Chapter IX

CROSS YOUR HEART

Many brilliant scientists have been involved with agencies of the United States Government on numerous projects of national concern. Some have worked to stop the spread of contagious disease, others have helped in our ventures into space, and some have worked in strategic areas critical to our defense. One such scientist was a naturalized British citizen on loan to the United States to work at the Los Alamos facility in New Mexico, an operation which, among other functions, is responsible for much of the past and current work on nuclear weaponry.

During his time in the United States he became a friend of David Greenglass who had recently been transferred from his assignment as a member of the US Army. The two worked on related projects, primarily aimed at improving detonation devices for the plutonium bomb.

David's wife Ruth was a friend of a young woman named Ethel from "back east" and often talked to her about their life in New Mexico. Along with her husband and his new British friend, she and the Greenglasses often socialized together, swapped stories together, laughed at the same jokes, and attended the same party. Oh, and by the way, the party they attended was the Communist Party. The Brit was a self-exiled German, Klaus Fuchs, loyal to communist doctrine. The time was 1944, Ethyl's husband was Julius (as in Rosenberg), and one of the most devastating lies ever to affect the world was being perpetrated.

It seems the United States and British governments were more concerned with certain objectives of gaining nuclear supremacy than worrying about a few scientists that had openly declared their belief in communism; the basic foundation of the Russian government. In fact, Hollywood was encouraged to make movies portraying life in Russia in a positive way, since they were an ally of ours during the war. As you may know, several years after WW2 this group of liars and traitors were discovered for what they were, and Ethel and Julius Rosenberg, ring leaders of a large contingency of US-based spies, were convicted and executed.

As the solicitors and conduits of highly secret information, they bore the brunt of punishment for the many years of deception. Lies that led to Russia constructing their own version of the atomic bomb, and establishing the basis for the "cold war" that lasted more than a generation. These were the lies that eventually brought the USSR and the United States to the brink of thermonuclear winter over the Cuban Missile Crisis. And these lies diverted vast economic resources of the US and Russia into both offensive and defensive military buildups, away from more humanitarian projects that by now may have resulted in the cure of cancer, development of new sources of clean energy, or lifted the socioeconomic levels of millions around the globe.

We will never know how the world would have been different. But what we do know is that even the lies of a few people can have tremendous and lasting consequences.

The stories of both the new and old testament are marked by incidents of lies and falsehoods. They are held up as examples of what terrible acts man can perpetrate on other men when the truth takes a back seat to deceit.

Inspired writers of the Bible realized the importance of honesty and trust. So much so that in the first few pages of the Bible, they quickly related the story of how the serpent deceived Eve and then Adam, into eating from the tree of knowledge; something they had been commanded by God not to do. Again, just a few sentences later in Chapter 4, Cain, after killing his brother Abel, is asked by God in verse 9, *"Where is your brother Abel?" "I don't know,"* he replied, *"Am I my brother's keeper?"*

It's hard to imagine Cain thought such a lie would be believed by God. Not only was he a murderer, he was stupid as well. And what about us? Do you think you've been fooling God too?

Even Peter, a Disciple of Christ, lied three times on the eve of the Crucifixion and fulfilled the prophecy that Jesus had stated *"Before the rooster crows, you will disown me three times"*- Matthew 26:75. Through his deceit, Peter protected himself from possible harm.

According to a psychologist, Gerald Jellison of the University of South California, we humans are presented about 200 deceptions every day . . . most of which we are never aware.

Lies come in all shapes and sizes. They are disguised as truths, hitch rides on legitimate stories, are buried inside statistical reports, and can be worn as easily as an article of clothing. For some they come easy, like water off a duck. For others, the mere thought of fabricating the truth causes a marked change in their physiology.

This latter problem forms the basis for many of the so-called lie detector machines. They are able to measure changes in blood pressure, heart rate, eye dilation, depth of breathing, skin conductivity, and other signs that often unmask a liar when tested.

Have you ever wondered why the body reacts so much to telling a lie? Maybe it's trying to tell *you* something as well.

Dr. James Dobson in his book "Parenting Isn't For Cowards", refers to Psalm 51:5 when King David says, *". . . in sin did my mother conceive me."* As he interprets this, Dobson states, *"Therefore, with or without bad experiences, a child is naturally inclined toward rebellion, selfishness, dishonesty, aggression, exploitation, and greed. He does not have to be taught these behaviors."*

We are all liars in one fashion or another - some more, some less. It is in our genes and as some scientists believe, was placed there as a basis for self-defense by our maker. And man is not alone in this trait. Some species of birds will fain injury to detract predators from their young. Certain fish will swallow large amounts of water and inflate themselves to twice their normal size to threaten their enemies or impress their prospective mate. And some animals like the squid will change it's skin coloration to match the background of is current habitation. Do you see some similarities to man?

I saw a person a few months ago that I had worked with many years earlier. He was a well-respected sales manager, leading a young group of type "A" folks starting a new dot com company. Mark (not his real name) was standing in the middle of an exhibit room enthusiastically explaining to a couple of his new charges how to sell their latest software product. As I walked up to him, something seemed a bit different.

He had always had a thin athletic build, spoke with a distinctive North Carolina accent, and had a commanding presence wherever he went. He also enjoyed a full, thick head of hair, even for being over fifty. But what I finally noticed was that the once medium brown hair, lightly streaked with gray only 10 years earlier, was now an even "Clairol'ed" chocolate.

Knowing Mark as well as I did, I couldn't help later re-marking to him that since I had seen him last, *"Richard Nixon wasn't the only person to have perpetrated a cover-up"*. He laughed and told me that when he inter-viewed for the position, he was afraid that the manage-ment of this company might view him as being too old for the job. Since the average age of the employees was thirty-one, he felt he needed to look closer to their age rather than one of their father's. Not only had he physi-cally repackaged himself, he had even tried to indoctrinate his brain with the latest music and slang, watching count-less hours of MTV. Although I laughed at the time, later in my hotel room I thought about how often we feel in-clined to deceive those around us. Maybe as a society we even expect it, perpetuate it, and discriminate against those who do not fit into the world, as we perceive it should be.

Later, I thought how much easier it would be to face real-ity if it were not for the expectations, right or wrong, of those around us.

There is a fine line between perception and deception.

Is it OK to intentionally create a perception of something other than what it really is or is that just another type of lie?

I remember an example of mistaken "identities" a few years ago when managing national alliances for a com-pany involved in Internet branding. Many of the organiza-tions I worked with were companies primarily providing web-based creative services, some seeing themselves as the glitz and glamour of the new communication age. Of-ten they were an offshoot of established public relations or advertising agencies like Sachi and Sachi or Olgivy and

Mather. Sometimes they were new companies with trendy names like iXL, Viant, or Razorfish.

On my first visit to New York to call on some of the organizations which inhabited an area of Manhattan nicknamed "Silicon Alley", I found myself sitting in a waiting room (painted all black with a couple of spinning lights overhead) dressed in my banker's gray suit, white shirt and rep tie. I noticed a couple of people passing in the outer hall and looking my way. A few minutes later, someone walked in the room and said, *"Are you looking for XYZ Law offices? They're just across the lobby."* I politely said no and told them who I was waiting to see. My appointment, as the receptionist had explained earlier (after she coerced me into having a cup of expresso) was running late from lunch.

As I continued to sit there, other people came into the reception area to wait on their appointments. It soon became obvious I was not dressed like anyone else. Most were wearing dark colored shirts, black pants, maybe a dark leather sport coat, ties that blended with the background (if they wore one), and shoes that looked more like a cross between bed room slippers and those made for jogging on a pauper's budget.

It wasn't long before I felt compelled to get an entirely new wardrobe to "fit in". That was about 10 years ago. Recently, I donated a number of the shirts and ties to a charity, no longer feeling comfortable in wearing them and not really sure anyone else would either. (I did keep some in case there is a costume party or "new age" retro contest in a few years).

I am reminded of David, prior to being King, pretending to be mentally disturbed in order to save his skin when he was recognized in an unfriendly territory. 1 Samuel 21:13, *"So he pretended to be insane in their presence; and while he was in their hands he acted like a madman, making marks on the doors of the gate and letting saliva run down his beard."*

I sometimes think I was temporarily insane, based on the trouble I went to trying to blend into a business territory alien to me. What ridiculous games we play!

Lies are propagated for many reasons and "fitting in" is certainly one excuse, poor though it is.

In sales and marketing, I have often heard the legal term "caveat emptor" quoted in regard to some new claim or invention. Translated from Latin it means, *buyer beware.* Here in the South, my mother's version was, *"Be careful not to buy a pig in a poke".*

Around every corner, in every mailbox, and through all types of electronic messages are traps ready to spring on our minds, souls, and pocketbooks. Even some of what we may have considered the most reputable of organizations are trying to snare us surreptitiously.

Why is it that phenomenal advertising claims are often footnoted with microscopically labeled disclaimers. Do you really think they want you do read them? If so, then why make them so small and, if on a television screen, why display them for such a short time that no human could possibly finish reading them before the image was replaced by something else?

Unfortunately in the world in which we live today, as in the time of Christ, we must constantly maintain a vigil not to be deceived. Yet, the many shades of deception make the challenge of being lied to, and our unwitting involvement, extremely difficult to overcome . . . particularly if we are, as the psychologist Jellison offers, confronted several hundred times a day.

*The "snake oil" vendors of the past are still alive
and well. They're just dressed in
more sophisticated guises.*

It is good to periodically remind ourselves of an old Yiddish Proverb that states, *"A half truth is a whole lie."* Unfortunately, most of us give and get them too frequently. Look at the billions of dollars that have been stolen from the rich and not-so-rich, by the likes of Enron Corporation when it was found, in 2001, they were "cooking the books", eventually filing for bankruptcy; costing many trusting individuals their livelihood or life savings from investing in the company.

Today, hard as it is to believe, there are countless individuals and groups, with the intent of recasting history. With a bit of research, you can find two such examples . . . the "Leuchter Report" and the "Remer Report". In these documents, the writers indicate that gas chambers were not used to murder Jews during WW2 as most books "incorrectly" describe, and that the majority of incarcerated died because of other diseases, which were generally unavoidable, or of malnutrition because of shortages of food and medicine due to Allied bombing.

These "Revisionists" apparently want to deceive us in order to cover the embarrassing reality, hopeful with time their fabricated tale will become the "truth". What a sad and misshapen thought process, and yet if we are complacent, things like this can and will happen.

~

Think how much more effort is used in lying.

If you lie, you have to remember things that never occurred where as telling the truth requires no preplanning or rehearsal or trying to keep mental notes of fictitious events. It is no wonder that on cross-examination, the stories being told by criminals often begin to come apart because the fabricated details cannot be repeated the same each time. How would you fair if you were on trial?

Prevarication, untruths, mis-spoken facts, fabrication of truths, intentional mis-statements, . . . if it looks like a duck, walks like a duck, quacks like a duck, then maybe it is a duck (or in this example a "lie")

The Politicians, like others, have chosen to water-down the nouns and adjectives for lying. They will go to extremes not to use the apparently unsociably acceptable word. I have not researched the specifics from a legal standpoint, but maybe you're more likely to be sued for slander if you use the words "lie" or "liar". Frankly, I think the real reason is that the short three letter word "lie" has so much significance and certainly needs no interpretation, that people are afraid to say it because of the strong moral resonance it has (or because it strikes too close to home).

If we lived on a planet 50 light years from Earth, with the proper television receiver, we could watch broadcasts of shows as they originally aired live 50 years in the past. As I write this part of the book that would be the late 1950's. There would be the vintage shows with Lucille Ball and Desi Arnez, or early morning kids programs like "Howdy Doody".

How is that possible?

It would take that long for the television signals to reach that distant planet because, traveling at the same speed of light, some 186,000 miles per second, the TV signal would take those 50 years to get there. It's like throwing a rock into the middle of a pond. The waves move out in all directions, being stronger at first, but diminishing in size and amplitude, until they finally reach shore; or in the case of television signals, another heavenly body.

Lies are a lot like those television broadcasts or waves in the water. They are strong at first, lose their significance over time, but continue to travel on until they reach other human "shores". It may be a few minutes, a few days, or even hundreds of years. One big problem is that once lies are told, you can't "untell" them. As one person remarked, *"Once the bell has rung, you can't get the ring back!"*

Children often tell all types of exaggerated stories in order to become the center of attention, or be part of the crowd. Some never grow out of the habit but rather become experts at creating illusions of reality.

When we were little, and we really wanted to confirm that we were telling the truth, some of us would finish our story by saying, "cross my heart and hope to die",(if you find I'm telling a lie). I'm glad that oath didn't work because I would never have gotten out of grade school. But, what if that oath always worked without exception AND we were required to say it whenever someone doubted what we were telling them? I bet the few people left on this planet would choose their words very, very carefully!

Lies are like daggers. They penetrate the soul when they are discovered, cut the cords of trust with our friends and associates, and create wounds within our moral fiber that mend slowly.

Lies are indicative of our fear to tell the truth. They are the easy way out of facing reality.

Recognizing the truth and telling the truth has to be two of the greatest challenges we face every day. On one side our guard must be raised high to avoid being a victim of someone's lies and on the other hand we must keep to our faith to avoid creating victims ourselves. Only with God's help and an allegiance to what we know is the truth can we succeed.

There is no such thing as a little lie.

Yes, some lies are worse than others, and maybe there are circumstances that justify lying when self preservation is an issue, but the principles by which they deceive are the same.

Those waves of deceit will continue to travel in an ever expanding circle, like the ripples from the rock thrown in the pond. You'll never know what shores they will eventually bump against, nor the destruction they may have. For a drug addict, once you start down the path of addiction, it is very difficult to stop. I think it is the same with lies . . . don't you?

Study Guide – Chapter IX
Cross Your Heart?

Lies come in all forms. As you think about situations you face each day, spend time evaluating each point as it relates to being untruthful with individuals or groups of people with whom you cross paths. Remember that lies go by many names or are propagated by lie-like actions. Examples would include exaggeration, half-truths, intentional misdirection, deceit, and re-interpretation of facts to increase someone's advantage over another.

1. *Try and think about the last time you told a lie and how you justified it in your mind. Could you have avoided this and, if so, how?*

2. *When you find that someone has lied to you, how does it make you feel about that person? Are you less trusting?*

3. *Have you ever lied and then been confronted with the truth? How did you feel and how did you excuse your actions? If Jesus were standing in front of you, could you have told the lie and, if not, why?*

4. *What is the best way to avoid telling a lie?*

5. *In the old story of the boy who cried wolf, what were his motives? Have you been deceitful for similar reasons?*

Group Discussion

1. *For those that are engaged or married, describe the last time you lied to your partner and relate the result.*

2. *Discuss an instance when various members of the group think a lie is justified (if ever).*

3. *Think of a politician or celebrity that was caught in a lie and discuss the repercussions when found out. Was the outcome to society damaged by their actions? Were individuals hurt by what they did? What effect was there (or could have been) on children?*

4. *Since many advertisements to which we are exposed are misleading, (although legally worded to avoid suits), how can we as individuals prevent being deceived by them? An example would be "Come on in this weekend and buy a car; good credit, weak credit, no credit . . . no application will be refused." Of course what they really mean is that you can fill out a credit application for a car and give it to them for evaluation, but it does not mean they will approve it. Yet that is what they want you to think! Their primary motive is to get you to their dealership.*

5. *Jesus is often credited with starting some of his statements with, "I tell you the truth . . .". Why would he say that? (ex. John 8:58) Was there a time Jesus did not tell the truth or did He intend something else by making this an introduction to His words?*

Chapter X

ARE YOU IN THERE?

Every culture on earth has basic staples, some more diverse than others. However, there is one natural food that
has constituted part of man's diet most likely since he has
walked this earth. Recorded history has indicated it was
cultivated in Egypt as early as 3500 BC; grown in large
fields by the Samarians by 2500 BC; and described in a
medical treatise by a famous Indian doctor in the 6th century BC as good for the digestion, the heart, the eyes, and
the joints.

What I found most interesting is that the Greeks, prior to
an athletic competition such as the Olympics, ate this food
raw, drank it's juices, and rubbed it all over their bodies.
How much of this food do you guess we individually consume each year?

On average, approximately 18 pounds is eaten annually by
Americans, but Libyans, who eat an estimated 66 pounds
each year, consume the most per person of all. By the way,
its medicinal properties, as described by the middle east-
ern cultures thousands of years ago have been proven true
by modern man. In fact, this miracle food can reduce the
chance of heart attacks, decrease the bad LDL cholesterol,
and destroy harmful bacteria in our mouth. During the
time of the Crusades, it was listed as one of the top three
foods eaten by the common man in Europe.[15]

Are there any down sides? Well, if you want to be close to
the one's you love, there may be some problems, because
with all of it's wonder and power, we know this food as the
"onion"!

The Romans called it "unio" meaning large pearl. Later, in Middle English about 400 years ago, it was phonetically pronounced the same as today although spelled "unyon". Regardless of what you call it, or the different varieties that have evolved, it is one of the most widely harvested food crops on earth, being able to be grown most any time of the year as long as the temperature stays above 20 degrees Fahrenheit.

Even the children of Israel remembered this "pearl" as they moved forward toward the Promised Land. They obviously missed having it when they complained to Moses about only getting "manna" to eat, *We remember the fish we ate in Egypt at no cost - also the cucumbers, melons, leeks, onions, and garlic.*"(Numbers 11:5)

Interestingly, the Egyptians valued the onion not only for food and medicinal purposes, but used it as a symbol to represent eternity because of the way its concentric layers seemed to go on and on. Peel back one, and there was another, and then another, until you finally reach the core. Except, in the case of the onion, there really is no core like a fruit, but just one final concentric layer.

Yet, from that one middle layer sprouts the strength of the plant when it is first growing. And with each new green leaf that grows up from the onion bulb, through the soil, and into the sun will come one more layer. Six green leaves means six layers, eight green leaves - eight layers . . .etc.

An onion makes a great metaphor of a man's life. As children first entering the light of day, we are like the core of the onion. The light and nourishment we receive from our environment let's us add more layers. And the more layers we add, the greater the chance of changing who we started out to be.

With the right care, we can grow and flourish in a way that is acceptable to God and to those around us. But let us get the wrong nourishment, and we may change into something unpalatable by all we meet. So, what kinds of layers do you have?

I think love is the first layer we add. Paul, in his letter to the church in Corinth spends the entire 13th chapter on love. In 13:2 he states, ". . . *and if I have a faith that can move mountains, but have not love, I am nothing*". And at the end of that chapter, in verse 13, in comparing faith, hope and love he writes, "*But the greatest of these is love*".

If we send up a leaf into the world, and find a place filled with our parent's love, then we will develop a layer that will protect us, and form the foundation for our layer of faith. Other layers we need include morality, kindness, forgiveness, and openness.

For some these layers will be thin; for others they will be imperfect; and for still others they will be strong and pure. However many layers I have at the end of my life, no matter how many are added or removed along the way, I want faith to always be the outermost layer, protecting me from the negative influences of the world, yet, like a sieve, letting the good through to my core.

God is constantly challenging you and me to keep those layers from changing us into something we should not be. We all have seen a death or disability add a layer of sadness to someone's life. Or what about new-found wealth, adding a layer of "better-than-thou" attitude?

We also build layers of worldly possessions, layers of friends, of family, and of memories. But no matter how many layers we grow through the years, God will always see into our hearts, past all of the layers of life. As the writer of Daniel 2:22 states, "*He reveals deep and hidden*

117

things; He knows what lies in darkness and light dwells with him."

If we can't hide from Him, then why do we hide from others?

The core of who we started out to be is still there, buried deep inside. Unlike the spirit of a young child, as we've grown older our's may have been hidden, confused or dulled by the elements to which we've been exposed. At birth our core was direct, to the point, unable to tell a lie, unadulterated with hidden meanings, and innocent of wrong doings. It was honest, pure in action and hungry in thought.

I am reminded of a time when we lived in a downtown neighborhood in Atlanta called Brookwood Hills. It is a neighborhood that has, for most of its almost 100 years, been a wonderful place to live and raise families.

One day, not long after we moved there, and before we had children, I was enclosing a screened porch on the front of the house. A little boy from two homes down the street liked to come and watch me hammer and saw. Usually he would stand for long periods of time, changing positions only to see me work from another angle, rarely saying anything unless spoken to. One such time, as I stood at the edge of the porch, I happened to ask him, *"David, what are your parents doing?"* hoping to start a conversation.

Without changing his glance or blinking an eye, this four-year-old stated matter-of-factly, *"I don't know, I'm not there."* He was telling the unvarnished truth the only way he knew how to do at that young age. Yet, think how different it is when we get older. We not only tell things differently, we *hear* things differently.

One early Winter morning, Eric, our first born, came into our bedroom. He was just two or three years old and during the winter, the old heart-of-pine floors were always cold that time of year. As he stood at the foot of our bed, my wife Ellie said, *"Don't run around in your bare feet, you might get sick."*

He stopped for a moment, and then big tears started running down his cheeks. *"What's the matter?"* Ellie asked. *"I don't have <u>bear</u> feet,"* he said, *" I have Eric feet."*

How often do you sit and ponder the intent or meaning of someone's statement rather than accepting it at face value? Are we afraid? Have we been conditioned to think everyone has a hidden agenda? Is there this layer of mistrust we have grown over the years?

These layers we add during our life can protect us, strengthen or weaken us, hold us up, or, unfortunately, hide us.

Hiding seems to be in vogue today more than ever.

When we are kids, we played hide-and-seek all the time in friend's houses. We would often run and open closet doors and ask *"are you in there?"* as if we really expected to get an answer. For those of us hiding, we would make noises to distract the hunter from the hunted, and then pray we would not be found out. It seems that way with many people. They are hiding, and when we try to find out who they really are, we get either no answer at all, or ones that are misleading.

I have often used an example of an experience most of us have had.

Can you remember a time when calling someone you knew well, they answered the phone and did not immediately recognize your voice? How did they sound at first?

For a guy, I usually refer to it as their "big boy" voice. It is usually stilted, hard-edged, strongly spoken, and devoid of any emotion other than possibly a "what do you want" inflection. Yet, as soon as they realize who they are speaking to, there is an immediate change in the quality of their voice, becoming softer, friendlier, without the false and posturing tone that had existed moments earlier. Well . . . there's an example of one of those layers temporarily getting in the way of who they really are.

Wouldn't it be great if that layer never existed for anyone? Do you have this layer and if so, how thick is it? And, more importantly, is it really necessary? In the end, remember, God sees through it all anyway! Luke 12:2, *"There is nothing concealed that will not be disclosed, or hidden that will not be made known. What you have said in the dark will be heard in the daylight and what you have whispered in the ear in the inner rooms will be proclaimed from the roofs."*

The next time the phone rings, answer it as if it were a friend calling (even if it's an annoying telemarketer). Try talking to the fast food worker as if you've known them your whole life, and watch their reaction, listen to their voice, and see if their demeanor changes for the better.

~

Because onions retain such high concentrations of water, archeologists find virtually nothing to analyze when they survey the sites of previous civilizations. Trees, on the other hand, even when dead for many years, leave a "documented" history of their development.

You and I can look at a cross-section of a stump, or the end of a piece of lumber, and read its history. Every layer, or "ring",represents one year, indicating its success at living during that period of time. Obviously, wider rings indicate a better growing environment as compared to thinner layers. Wouldn't it be interesting if we could peer into the "rings" of those around us and quickly see which ones were successfully developed and which ones were not?

Onions have a number of different chemicals in them. Most are good for us. Adenosine causes the blood to thin, decreasing our blood pressure. Sulfur, in contrast, combines with the moisture in our eyes to cause them to sting by producing a mild solution of sulfuric acid. The level of sulfur in the onion's cells determines the intensity of how our eyes will react when we cut into them. Because onions have a tendency to store excess sulfur if available, it is best to grow them in neutral, well-drained soils, avoiding fertilizers with high concentrations of sulfur compounds.

Like the onion, if we place the wrong "fertilizers" and "soil" around our children or ourselves, when we "cut" into those layers, they will sting our eyes, heart and mind with pain. Look at the history of adults that grew up in homes filled with hate, abuse, deceit or neglect. Like high concentrations of sulfur in an onion, these people cannot help but give back what was put into them. But if we nurture them with love, kindness, truth and faith in God, they will grow and flourish accordingly. That way, when the layers are removed there will be no surprises, and we'll find the core as it was in the beginning.

Maya Angelou[16] once said, *"There is no greater agony than bearing an untold story inside you."* I would like to take that a step further by paraphrasing, *"There is no greater agony than finding that the story inside of you is much better than what is seen from the outside."*

Some day you will see the scowling face of someone next to you at a check-out counter, mad because they have had to wait a long time to be served. Do you think they were born looking that way? I know there are times that I would not want to look in the mirror as well . . . maybe it would be a good idea to carry one in our pockets for just such occasions. And certainly, like the onion, we may have visible layers that are battered or bruised, but often they can be removed to show the value and beauty that is inside.

Don't let the goodness and freshness of the spirit you were born with be so hidden that no one can find it!

Challenge yourself to let it be seen. Remember that one of the first expressions a baby makes is a smile . . . not a bad beginning point is it?

They say a good onion has a natural transparency to it. Light will easily penetrate its layers and give it a beautiful luminescence, as the Greeks so aptly named it, *like a pearl.* I would say the same about a good-spirited person . . . wouldn't you?

Study Guide – Chapter XI
Are You In There?

As humans we are prone to hide behind both real and imaginary shields. If we are honest with ourselves, and secure in our beliefs, then does it make sense to hide. Throughout the Christian Bible, we are challenged to honorably expose ourselves to God and to our fellow man or woman. Think about the challenges to do this as you consider each of the following:

1. *Has there been a recent instance where you failed to let someone know how you felt about something they said or did that was contrary to what you believe is correct or truthful? If so, why did you not speak out? Have you had any regrets since then?*

2. *Do you think it is alright to avoid a conflict by pretending to ignore hurtful words aimed at you or someone you know? Write down the why's and why nots.*

3. *Sometimes we act very differently around our children, spouses, and close friends as compared to total strangers. Why would you do that? Did a Disciple act that way once?*

Group Discussion

1. *Does group interaction encourage you to act differently than you would with your family, and if so, why?*

2. *How does God want you to represent yourself to others? (Read Psalm 15:2-5, Mark 10:23-25)*

3. *As we get older, how do we preserve the goodness and purity with which we were born?*

Chapter XI

OLD TIMBERS

Like any year filled with hundreds of significant and newsworthy events among many thousands of less conspicuous happenings, 1921 was no different.

One of the more notorious happenings was the "Black Sox" trial. Charles Comisky's 1919 Word Series baseball team was accused of having eight of their players "throw" (intentionally lose) the game by taking substantial bribes.

Another baseball event that occurred in 1921 was the first broadcast of a World Series game on radio. There was also the peace treaty with Germany signed three years after WWI ended, (but never by the United States). The Chinese Communist Party was formed; Warren Hardy became President; and Charlie Chaplin took a hand at directing his first movie (in which he also starred).

It was the beginning of the "roaring twenties", a time of prosperity, of expanding job markets, and the front-end of one of the largest decades of building the United States has ever seen.

Of much significance to our family, in 1921 our second home was built by a Mr. Bennett who gave it to his daughter as a wedding present. And after it had mellowed for fifty-five years, we happily took it as the third owner in 1976. I say "happily" because we had been like babes in the woods, when we had bought our first house three years earlier.

First, let me tell you about that previous house.

There seemed to have been a certain wonderment about buying that house, particularly since it was new. Later our wonderment turned into just plain wonder when we wondered why we had bought that home.

I will never forget the day, about two months after we had moved into the little one story house in Snellville, Georgia, when the contractor that had built the home dropped by. After gingerly getting out of his pickup truck, with a big grin on his face he asked, *"Hey, how do you like the house?"*

I said, *"Fine, why?"*

"Oh, it was the first house I ever built. I used to be a dry-wall contractor, but I figured I could make more money by building the whole thing."

Later, as I learned more about house construction, I decided he should have remained a dry-wall contractor!

When the first cold days of winter arrived, and our heating system never seemed to stop running, I discovered he had forgotten to put any insulation in the ceiling (*"just a little oversight"* he said when we called). Then when we decided to finish part of the basement for a recreation room, I noticed that many of the cross braces for the floor above were either missing nails, or were so short as to not reach between the joists they were supposedly bracing. (Often they were hanging in mid-air, suspended by a couple of nails on each end, or in some instances, I could swear they were floating by way of a magician's spell - not that there is such a thing as a "spell"). Of course, there was the leak in the basement wall because gutters had been misdirected and improper contouring of the yard directed water to run *toward* the house instead of away from it.

Of most concern was when, after putting the house on the market, one of our prospective buyers - a very nice lady but who was *very* much overweight - came to see the home. As she walked through our den, the floor would bow such that the furniture would lean away from the wall toward her. Maybe she was used to that happening, but I wasn't. Anyway, of all the people who came to see it, she was the one who made us an acceptable offer. The little house is still standing after 30 years, but certainly appears the worse for wear.

Our second home on Northwood Avenue in Atlanta stood in stark contrast to the first. There is something very secure in owning a home that has lasted for over 50 years. I think it comes from knowing that it must have been reasonably well built in the beginning, and had the proper "care and feeding" in various forms of maintenance through the years. Then there are all of the memories of laughter and joy, tears of happiness, tears of sadness, children's feet running, dogs' barking, and stolen kisses behind a door . . . all bound into its fiber. If only those walls could speak to us, imagine all they could say!

As we grow older, I think we begin to appreciate "oldness". (Maybe because it starts to look like us).

It's too bad that we do not take the time to appreciate older people when we are younger - a time in our lives when their experiences could be of such importance in shaping our future. Like our first home, we seem so anxious to associate ourselves with something new, we forget about the value of age. Mark Twain once said, *"When I was a boy of fourteen, my father was so ignorant I could hardly stand to have the old man around. But when I got to be twenty-one, I was astonished at how much he had learned in seven years."*

Most of us are taught to respect our elders at an early age. Somehow I think we forget that respect does not mean just to hold the door for them, say *"yes sir"* and *"no Mam"* to them, and serve them the first plate at the Thanksgiving dinner.

As a sophomore in college, I remember dating a girl at Agnes Scott College, whose family was from Thomaston, Georgia, a mill town in the middle part of the state. On Sunday after church (mandatory attendance even for visitors), we ate the noon meal in one of the dining rooms at the local hotel. Her grandmother was a devout Christian, having once been married to a very famous and widely published minister of the first half of the last century, H.A. Ironside. I will assure you, she not only commanded respect, but also by my observation, was always given it.

I still have a vivid memory of her sitting at the head of the long table, the newest grandchild stationed at her side in a highchair, no one being seated until she sat, and no one eating until she had passed the plates. She was, after all, the ruling matriarch of that large and extended family. But, regardless of position, I also felt they respected her opinion and advice, something missing from many families today, and we are worse-off because it is not there.

Within many societies, (unfortunately not as often in America), the elderly are always respected and valued for their wisdom. In very primitive cultures this seems extremely logical for if you were able to survive to an old age, by not falling prey to wild animals, being killed by other tribes, or eating only foods that were not poisonous, you were considered very wise indeed!

For the early Jewish and Christian families, this reverence and respect for their elders was very apparent *and* required. As part of the various laws, in Leviticus 19:32 it is spelled out, *"Rise in the presence of the aged, show respect for the elderly and revere your God."*

One of the few descriptions of Jesus as a child recounts how, like many children, he wandered off from his parents as they journeyed home. The family had been attending the annual Feast of the Passover in Jerusalem. When after three days of searching, his parents discovered he had gone to the temple. There Jesus had sat, listening to the elders, questioning them for knowledge, and preparing himself for his role in the Jewish community.

It was the tradition, that Jewish males after reaching the age of twelve, would spend time with the temple elders. Their age and accumulated wisdom was revered by most of the younger crowd. This passing of knowledge from the old to the young had existed as part of their culture for many generations.

The Bible seems relatively clear about following the wisdom of older folks. Those that ignored the advice of the elders seemed to come out on the losing end as with King Rehoboam when he rejected the advice of the aged counselors to his father, King Solomon.

Instead, as the elders had suggested, of being a servant to the Israelites, *"serve them and give them a favorable answer, (so) they will always be your servants,"* (1 Kings 12:7) he listened to those young, inexperienced men that had grown up with him. In order to gain the continued servitude of the Israelites, his buddies suggested making their life even worse than Solomon had imposed. Rehoboam's man Adoniram, who was in charge of forced labor, was soon stoned to death and Rehoboam barely escaped with his life by fleeing to Jerusalem.

There are certainly times I can remember when I ignored advice of people older than me and barely escaped with my life, both figuratively and literally.

Some people today believe that technology is diminishing what younger people see as the value of their elders. They think that Internet search engines, with just a few keystrokes, will provide all of the information they need. What they fail to realize is that information does not equate to experience nor can they talk to the computer to get the tone and emotion which can change the character of the words and wisdom.

Jesus, although wise beyond His years, never acted as if He were the supreme being and all knowing. He sought guidance from his Father many, many times and He made it clear to those around Him that His guidance came from God. As an example, in the last part of John 8:28, Jesus is quoted as saying, *"I do nothing on my own but speak just what the Father has taught me."* And He continues in verse 8:29, *"The one who sent me is with me; he has not left me alone, for I always do what pleases Him."* In other words, Jesus was not experimenting. He was being guided along His path, efficiently and effectively.

God is as old as the universe He has created. Who else is eldest among all of us, living or dead? Why would we not turn to Him and pray for guidance as did Jesus?

Eric Hoffer, an American philosopher and winner of the Presidential Medal of Freedom, wrote, *"Old age equalizes - we are aware that what is happening to us has happened to untold numbers from the beginning of time. When we are young we act as if we were the first young people in the world."* How many of us have and continue to act that way? In my heart, I know it was one of the problems that separated me from really knowing my father.

Although he came from a much different environment from the one in which I grew up, as the son of a country farmer and nurseryman he became a reasonably successful entrepreneur in Atlanta. He, along with my mother who enjoyed a career most of my childhood, provided our family with a good, secure middle-class life and my sister Janet and I never seemed to be in want of food, spending money, or wheels.

Unfortunately, I was never one for taking my father's advise, thinking I was smarter, more knowledgeable about the world, and able to cope without his help. Our disagreements often seemed to be about everything and at the same time, nothing of true importance. Frequently they centered around politics, philosophy, or culture, but even things like cars, houses, investments or how to use a particular tool were fair game. This friction prevented me from sharing in his life, understanding what had driven him to start several successful businesses, and even knowing who he truly was.

Today, as I write this, I am sorry that I did not take the time to ask him those questions that now haunt my mind. It's much too late, and it's my fault.

Would he have told me that the best life is one where you are your own boss? Could he have shown me what to look for in a loyal employee? And, how did he happen to have a partner in business that came from a noted Atlanta family, and was so far removed from my father's background on a farm?

These are questions, that for the most part, will never have an answer.

~

Having an old house did require me to perform more maintenance than a newer home might have dictated.

Once, while trying to scrape some peeling paint around what we had assumed for six years to be a false fan light about the front door, we made a surprising discovery. My tool had slipped, hitting one of the black-painted "wooden" panes with a loud "click" rather than the expected "thud".

My curiosity led me to begin furiously scrapping more paint until after about two hours, I had unmasked five glass panes. Two more hours passed, and I had broken through from the inside to reveal the entire fan light, obviously covered over at the last moment, toward the end of the home's construction.

Later that week, I built the necessary moulding to trim and frame it, and for many more years we enjoyed the light it provided into the living room and on certain Winter days, when it streamed down the central hall to give the core of the house a warm glow.

I can't imagine why anyone wanted to have that window closed off. But it reminds me that many older people have windows into their experiences, their wisdom, and their spiritual core that may have become blocked off. Maybe they did it . . . or more likely, maybe we did it to them.

When we had owned that house for about ten years, we decided to expand it by adding a second story. The do-it-yourselfer that I am, I drew the plans, got the approval of the city and historical oversight committees, secured a general contractor, and off we went. About four months later, we had almost doubled the size of our little home.

Because of the time when the house was built, and because the house had been constructed by the developer as a gift for his newly-married daughter, the foundation and timbers in its construction were extraordinary.

For example, true (dimensional) 4 X 10 inch beams (those are huge by today's standards) ran the width of the structure, resting on walls constructed of granite rocks and cement, with additional support pillars of 6 X 8 timbers, a few feet apart. When we added the tremendous weight of a second story, they held up very well with no settling. What we did not know at the time was that most of the outer wall supports had been destroyed decades earlier by termites.

Because the downstairs had been finished in the 1920's to serve as maids' quarters, we never thought to look on the other side of the wall coverings, but when we sold it, the new buyers did. What a surprise! Luckily for us, those central timbers had been so strong that they had carried the entire 3600 square foot structure much like a pedestal for a tabletop. You could take a pencil and push it through the remnants of the few remaining perimeter wall studs and sills. (As you can imagine, all of the outer walls were reinforced as a requirement before we closed the sale).

But, like that old house, if we look beyond the gray hair, or liver spots, the wrinkled skin, or the slow movement, we will probably find strong timbers of wisdom in our elders that can serve us well, support us, and provide many years of comfort and direction.

They say when buying a house, try to look past the apparent cosmetic problems for the value underneath. Isn't it the same for most people - young and old, rich or poor?

I can still remember the youth in my Grandfather Stalvey's bright and bluest of eyes. I can still hear my wife's dad, Joe Greene, explaining one of his obtuse jokes at the dinner table. My Uncle M.D.'s deep southern drawl still resonates as I remember him retelling one of his fishing or hunting stories. I can still hear my father laugh when, surprisingly, he became Santa Claus one night for a community Christmas event, when the original designated dad became sick. And, I can still remember my mom's stories of her youth and moving over 200 miles to Atlanta at seventeen, to pursue a career in the big city. I wish they were still here on earth so I could ask them some questions I should have asked earlier.

Don't wake up some day and discover that you have wasted much of your life running into walls that others, much older and wiser, have already figured out how to avoid.

God gives you the choice to learn again or learn anew.

The tough challenge is to put your ego and youthfulness aside and to seek guidance from those that have gone before you . . . make your life one of adding to, rather than one of repetition.

Marie Dressler, a Canadian-born actress who began in films at age 45 in 1914, and appeared in over 25 movies once said, *"By the time we hit fifty, we have learned our hardest lessons. We have found out that only a few things are really important. We have learned to take life seriously, but never ourselves.* To that I would add, for many of us our faith in God, our family, our friends, and our memories are the few things that are really important. Take advantage of them now. Even waiting another hour or day could be too late.

Seek the old timbers for their guidance because they are all around you; look for them in your Bible; and put their wisdom in your soul for you too, will hopefully be an old timber some day.

Study Guide – Chapter XI
Old Timbers

1. Make a list of five people you know who you would con-sider substantially older than yourself. For each one write at least one open-ended question you would like to ask them, and then go do it in the next five days. Write down (or record) their answers and also how they responded emo-tionally (happy, enthusiastic, etc.) Afterward, evaluate how their answers could affect you in the future? Did you get more information than you expected, and if so, why?

2. How can your involvement with "old timbers" help you? Write down as many as you can. If you believe in even one, doesn't it make sense to continue seeking conversations with them?

3. How can your involvement with "old timbers" help them? Again, make a list. If there is only one point in the list, then you probably already know what to do.

Group Discussion:

1. Find two places in the Bible where Jesus sought the help of God and discuss His rationale.

2. Discuss why, unlike many other countries, older people in the United States are not given as much respect.

3. Ask each person to relate a story of how someone, at least thirty years their senior, positively affected their lives at any time in the past.

4. Did Jesus relate to his followers as someone who was in his thirties or as someone much older? Explain.

Chapter XII

HOW DEEP?

The Earth is not a solid structure. We walk on what is commonly referred to as the "Crust" which floats on a semi-liquid mantle composed mostly of dense materials like iron, other metals, and silica. This reasonably hard layer varies in depth from about 20 km(12 miles) in continental land masses to about 8 km (4 miles) under the ocean. It forms an extremely thin shield between all living things on or near the surface of the earth and the approximately 5000 km of hot molten material not far below our feet (only about an hour's drive on an expressway). At the deepest levels of this inner layer, the liquid mass moves around a final solid iron core, and in the process, creates the magnetic fields of the Earth. Once in a while, the Earth's crust springs a leak and the hot molten rock and minerals flow out as lava.

Amazingly, man has never been able to drill through this outer crust.

The deepest *hand-dug* hole was excavated in 1887 in Greensburg, Kansas and was turned into a tourist attraction in 1939. It was only 109 feet deep and 32 feet in diameter. The Chinese claim to have reached depths of approximately 2500 feet using some type of elaborate bamboo pole, rope and metal tool contraption, in order to reach natural gas as fuel to heat salt water so as to retrieve the salt. Typical oil wells are about 10,000 - 16,000 feet deep, but some have been taken to a depth of almost 4 miles. The deepest drilled hole that my research found indicates a depth of about 12km (7 1/2 miles) in Murmansk Russia that was abandoned short of reaching through the Earth's crust to the mantle below.[17]

What you may find interesting is that water has occasionally been found in the rock at these great depths and more amazing is that single and multi-cell creatures have recently been discovered there too!

These creatures have found a way to survive even when faced with what appear to be overwhelming negative odds for life to exist.

~

Man has a great propensity for survival. As humans, we have the ability to find ways to survive even the most traumatic and depressing of situations. Yet, there are those times when we can also fail unless we get help from beyond our own self.

Instead of a hole in the ground, we can develop a deep metaphorical hole into which our spirit can fall.

For some, the hole is so deep that there is no return, yet, like the tiny creatures discovered at great depths in the ground, even under the most adverse circumstances, we can survive and be rescued.

I am reminded of the story of Daniel and how upon disobeying a decree of King Darius, he was thrown into the lion's den. Yet through his continued and unyielding faith, Daniel was saved by God and as described in Daniel 6:23" *. . . And when Daniel was lifted from the den, no wound was found on him, because he had trusted in his God.*"

Man, among all of God's creatures is the only species that is known to have the innate potential to intentionally take their own life. Yes, there are instances where a wild animal, brought into captivity, refuses to eat and ultimately dies of starvation. And, there are stories of pets that seem to become heartbroken and die soon after their master's life ends.

Humans are different. We, unfortunately, have the ability to not only pick the time, but the method by which we can destroy ourselves. It is but one of several possible conclusions to living with depression. Only today as I write this, the news media reported the suicide of a well known neighborhood restaurant owner. The jovial, warm-hearted man had often greeted my family at the door of his pizza place. Never could I have guessed some day he would take his life.

Another person I knew for several years in the software industry, took his life when he became depressed over family matters. He could not face the prospect of his children being hundreds of miles away, after his ex-wife decided to move to another part of the country. His selfish act has deprived his children of their father, and deprived those who worked with him of his great smile, generosity, and friendship.

He had called me only a few days earlier and left a voice mail about getting together for lunch. For several weeks after he died, I replayed that message over and over, never once detecting even the slightest hint of anxiety or emotional stress. On the surface he seemed to be the same cheerful person as I had always known. I often think of his smile and laughter.

~

The National Institute of Mental Health is quoted as saying that in 2004, suicides was the 11th leading cause of deaths in the United States. According to the Centers for Disease Control, suicides on average account for approximately 89 deaths in the United States every day, or one every 16 minutes. This is a staggering number when you consider it is classed as a preventable form of death.

Suicide rates vary widely from country-to-country around the world. A number of organizations track these statistics, including the World Health Organization. The latest, at the time of this publication is from October 2008. Of those with relatively current information, Lithuania leads with 68.1 males and 12.9 females per 100,000 population per gender, per year. while the United States numbers are 17.1 and 14.5 respectively.

Without doing a detailed analysis, there are some generalities that appear when looking at the data. Countries that are located further away from the equator have a much higher rate (3-4 times) as those in much warmer climates. Russia and many of the ex-Soviet countries have some of the highest incidence of suicide. And, women, regardless of country, are far less likely to take their lives; (with a few exceptions), roughly 25% as many compared to males.

Taking just the information on females, could the lower suicide rate be due to their traditional roles as caretakers for other members of their family, an obligation most take both seriously and without complaint. Or could it be the result of a stronger commitment to their faith which is supported by a number of surveys? I suspect it's a composite of both with the majority weighted toward the latter; in other words, their faith in God.

As examples, the latest government statistics for Great Britain (National Center for Social Research - www.statistics.gov.UK) in 1999 indicate that 10% of males and 13% of females practice their religion on at least a weekly basis. In the United States, even less men as a percentage, attend Church regularly, regardless of marital status or ethnicity according to a poll conducted from 1998-2002 by PBS.org, with the general difference being about 8 percentage points.

~

I would like to believe that everyone who becomes clinically depressed could be saved from either physical or mental self-destruction. The reality is that some will not make it.

Through our ongoing research, we know that chemical imbalances within our bodies can increase our likelihood to become depressed. Medicines like Paxil, Zoloff, and Prozac have shown some success at blocking the effects of those naturally produced, but harmful, chemicals. Surprisingly, some of the pharmaceutical manufacturers even state they do not know exactly how their products work. What they see is positive emotional changes within their patients, and assume it was the result of the medication.

Yet, with all of these new drugs, we are only fighting a catalyst within the soul of the person that generates their emotional imbalance. Our manmade solutions mask more deep-seated causes rather than remedy the problem.

It seems that too frequently we offer people a pill as the solution rather than finding a positive prescription for their life.

Although doctors will often treat the symptoms, a good consultant will tell you that the only true solution can come by discovering the root cause of the problem. It is no different with depression.

Although depression manifests itself in many ways, several people I know who have battled it have given me surprisingly similar descriptions. To paraphrase, *"It is like falling into a deep well where the light is dim, the walls seem insurmountable, and no matter which way you look, your mind becomes confused by the sameness surrounding you. There is a feeling of hopelessness that permeates your thoughts and tramples your spirit."*

Depression can make victims of not only the carrier, but of those around them. Families can be destroyed, businesses ruined, and the breath of life stolen away. It is a challenge God puts before some of us in small ways and for others as very deep chasms from which they or their friends must climb out. Ultimately, it is a selfish act and wastes the God-given abilities we could use to benefit others. On the other hand, even those that see a purpose for their life often feel they cannot achieve their goals because they are constantly beaten down by their environment. They begin to lose hope.

The book of Job certainly describes one man's torment and despair as he tried to cope with what seems insurmountable calamities in his life. In Chapter 3, verses 1-13 he expresses his feelings by essentially wishing he had never been born or that he were dead, *"For now I would be lying down in peace; I would be asleep and at rest."* v.13.

I can imagine that people living in an oppressed society as was the old Soviet empire (USSR), where freedom of religion was not allowed, could easily become saddened and depressed. And with the difficulties of practicing their faith, stood a better chance of losing it. What a tremendous challenge they had placed before them!

Wasn't it the same for the early Christians, when their leaders were killed or imprisoned? And yet, much like Christianity eventually threw off the shackles that bound them, so did the peoples of the old Soviet Union. Today Churches, Synagogues, and other places of worship have had a rebirth throughout the countries once comprising the USSR and I suspect the suicide rates will decline as a result.

~

I have been blessed to have never been deeply depressed or saddened for any long period of time. But when melancholy strikes, I have found the best medicine to come from one of three sources - my family, my friends, and my Bible. The one which is most readily available and always reliably there is God's written word. There are so many inspirational stories and verses that it would be hard not to find one by just randomly opening to any page.

Although I believe certain medications can aid in the relief of depression, as I said earlier, a true and lasting solution can best be delivered by a faith-based remedy. As with all prescriptions, the right measure delivered over a long period is usually required for optimum results.

Taking a dose of God daily is much more effective than a sporadic capsule of faith.

For individuals I have known with ongoing bouts of depression, those whose faith was strong, and whose trust in God was clear, seem to have the strongest desire to sustain their life, and continue to climb out and stay out of the deep hole in which they found themselves. Their success is a testament to the will of God through their belief in Him.

It is also an affirmation that God teaches us to be more concerned about others than ourselves; to reach out rather than spiraling inward. Again, maybe one reason women's rates of suicide are much lower is because they devote much of their lives to helping their family.

Think how much harder will it be for us to take the selfish path to destruction if we are taking a selfless road toward the world in which we live!

Getting involved in activities that promote the work of God through visible and sustainable projects is one way in which you or others can avoid falling victim to depression.

There are literally hundreds of groups, many in most every community, that afford the opportunity to give of one's self. Habitat for Humanity, Christmas in April, The Junior League, Rotary Club, and Scouting programs are but a few of the ones in which most can participate.

Why do you think retirement homes often have activities for their occupants that include the making of tangible objects such as jewelry, candles, flower arrangements, etc.? Years of experience has shown that stimulating the mind through the process or creation lifts the spirits and brings value to their lives and others around them.

~

The deeper one falls into depression, just like the hole in the ground, the light at the top gets dimmer and dimmer. It's an interesting phenomenon that the human body needs light in order to produce certain chemicals to lift the spirit and repel depression. Seasonal Affective Disorder (SAD), for example, is a condition most noted in regions of the world where in the winter, too little natural light causes depression within some groups of people.

The pineal gland, which is stimulated when light hits the retina at the back of your eye, causes the production of melatonin, a natural chemical which among other things, helps regulate emotion. By using very bright (above 2500 lumens) florescent lights whose frequency more closely mimics that of natural sunlight, people spending a few minutes or hours a day in front of them often have the symptoms of depression decrease substantially or completely disappear.

The Bible is one way to provide light for us. It illuminates our soul and brightens our path.

If, like Daniel, we stay dedicated to God and his word, at least that light will shine for us when all others go out. We need to act like those with SAD and sit in the intense light of God's word. We should challenge ourselves to be aware of those who need this light and then offer it to them. Sometimes the ones who need help most are least able to ask for it, or . . . even recognize the need.

We also can "worry" ourselves into a feeling of depression or sadness. Sometimes it's nothing more than evaluating an event using the "glass is half empty" approach rather than seeing it as the "glass is half full". Jesus, almost humourously states in Matthew 6:27, *"Who of you by worrying can add a single hour to his life?"* And, as we know medically, worry and stress can actually shorten your life span.

On a recent CBS news program discussing the 65th anniversary of "D Day",(the date Allied Forces in World War II invaded the coast of Normandy France), the anchor stated that approximately 1000 American Veterans of that war were dying weekly - most of old age. At first hearing this I felt sad, but then thought, *"wasn't it great that these people had lived into their 80's, had a chance to experience miraculous change in the world, and were able to celebrate the completion of a memorial to their courage and effort, finished only in the past few years?"* Some people only hear the sadness in such stories and never think of the positive aspects. Are you guilty of this?

~

As friends or family, saving someone from depression is one of the most important tasks you can do for God, because not only are you saving them, you may be saving others around them as well. And, in the act of preparing for this challenge, you may be saving yourself.

Think about it.

Study Guide – Chapter XII
How Deep?

Unfortunately, too many of us have known someone who has taken their life because of depression. In thinking about the following questions and points of discussion, try to determine the severity and effect of depression not only on the person directly troubled by their mental state, but on those around them.

1. What factors do you think (or have observed) can typically trigger depression? Are they often times preventable?

2. Have you or a close friend or relative, ever been tempted to take your own life because of being depressed? If so, what actions did you or someone else take to end that path to self-destruction? Was one of the steps reaching out to God for help? If not, why?

3. How should you as an individual help someone who is sad or deeply depressed? Make a list and then rank them in order of importance based on what you think would be most effective, and then do some research to see if you can confirm your thoughts quantifiably. A good start would be researching the Bible before turning to the Internet.

4. Do you think you have the preparation to help someone who is sad or depressed and if not, why?

Group Discussion

1. If anyone in your group has ever contemplated suicide, have them describe what led up to it if they are comfortable sharing their story. As an alternative, have each member relate similar circumstances about someone they know.

2. Ask the group if anyone knows why some religions believe it is a sin to commit suicide. If no one can answer, make it a topic for research before you meet again.

3. Considering how the story of Job is one of an innocent and God-fearing individual being bombarded by terrible incidents to everything he holds dear, read the advice he received in Chapter 5, verses 8-17. Discuss what is meant and how we would apply the counseling to our own lives.

4. Discuss positive outcomes where individuals have left depression behind them; how they have moved forward positively and survived.

5. Look for answers from group members to the following question, "When should someone reach out to God for help when they are feeling sad or depressed?"

6. Although global statistics support a general ratio of about 4 to 1, men to women, in regard to suicide, the ratio in the United States is closer to 1 to 1. Could this be due to women in the United States striving for more equality in the workplace, holding more full-time jobs, thus resulting in less time and devotion to their family and faith?

Chapter XIII

METAMORPHOSIS

The creation of human life is a phenomenon. It is the epitome of God's miracles, and was the beginning of the Christian faith through the birth of Jesus.

In the abstract, each conception is a starting over of thought and history and wisdom. And whether life is limited to this Earth, or as many speculate, repeated thousands of times in the universe, it is never-the-less an amazing event . . . and one we often take for granted.

There are all kinds of creatures on this planet, exemplifying both strange and astonishing methods of birth and development. On the surface, some are seemingly no more complex than single-celled animals giving rise to more single-celled animals. In other situations, as with the frog, one creature evolves to exist in a particular habitat only to give way to another form with an entirely different structure, better adapted to a new environment.

A tadpole, with its strong tail and insatiable appetite is able to quickly swim and gather food over a wide area, aiding its rapid growth and ability to become widely dispersed from the cluster of eggs from which it sprang. Later as a frog, it is able to leap its way over land in search of food, facing substantially different survival scenarios than in its previous form.

Then there are examples of animals that evolve to fit their localized environment, taking on the coloration of its habitat, mimicking other nearby creatures, or as in the case of some fish, adjusting growth and size to fit the physical constraints of its home.

As much as many of us hate to admit it, in various ways we are no different from many of the other creatures God has placed on Earth. We too have the tendency to fit into the world in which we find ourselves, often mimicking those around us and following in the footsteps of those that came before us. And as parents or guardians of some of the littlest forms of these Earthlings, God has placed both an emotional blessing and a difficult emotional challenge at our doorstep as part of that responsibility to make sure they mimic, then become, the best of what life should be.

~

A wide variety of scholars over the years have conducted extensive comparative studies to determine how humans develop. Today, many believe that as much if not more than 50% of our development and actions are determined by our genes . . . our physical heritage, blueprinted in each and every cell of our bodies. What a miracle it is that something as small as the DNA strands confined within the wall of our cells predetermine how we will be basically formed into a human being! The study of identical twins raised apart often demonstrates this clearly, when as adults they are found to be very similar both in appearance and action.

One television program many years ago documented how two twin brothers each, independent of the other, built a circular bench around a tree in their respective yards, although they had no contact with each other nor did they know at that time of the other's existence.

Doctors today now thankfully recognize that the risk of having certain types of diseases like cancer, or tendencies for high blood pressure, strokes, or birth defects, can be directly related to our lineage.

The inclination and propensity to do certain things in life seems to be preprogrammed into our metal. However, the other part of our development will be determined by our environment, and that is where God puts up the highest of hurdles for us to overcome.

On the one hand there can be no greater joy than to welcome a new child into our world. There is the sound of soft breathing as they sleep in your arms, the smoothness of their skin as you apply lotion to those unavoidable rashes, and the wonderment in all the little noises that only a baby can make. We get the privilege of seeing the first smile, listening to a first word, and watching the first shaky step. And if we are truly blessed, we get to see them become an adult.

The writers of the Bible spent little time describing the activities of Jesus as a child. I surmise it was because, after all, he was human and probably shared similar experiences as most children. Like all good parents, I feel sure that Mary and Joseph shared in those same types of events all of us as parents experience. I can imagine Jesus as a baby spitting-up on someone's cloak at the most inopportune time, or as a two-year old tugging one too many times on Mary's dress when he was ready to go and she was not. All of these are typical of the happy memories we place in our mind about our children.

Yet, inevitably as they grow we also must share in all of their troubles. We must listen to their cry of pain when they take their first hard fall, wipe away the big tears when their favorite toy is broken, or be saddened when they have their first fight with a playmate.

My oldest son Eric was prone to taking physical risks even at a very early age. I've lost count of the number of broken bones, but each and every time I felt his pain (and so did my billfold). Yet, I can still laugh when I think about him pitching a ball game more than twenty summers ago, with a cast on his leg.

Over one weekend, in separate incidents, both he and my other starting pitcher were injured. My son broke his ankle and the other boy, Justin, broke his arm. After trying a couple of other kids for two games (and losing both miserably), I got permission from the umpire to put Eric in as pitcher halfway through our next game. (Luckily for us my wife was busy with our other son that morning or I don't think I would have succeeded in this act of desperation).

The crowd roared as he placed the big heel of the walking cast behind the "rubber" on the pitcher's mound , pivoting on it as he threw the ball across home plate. Not surprisingly, I don't remember if we won, but we sure had fun trying!

Like weights on a scale, life's trials and tribulations always seem to balance our children's joys just as they do for us as adults. And like the good shepherd, we need to be there for them.

In our role as guardians of their physical well being, we must also be guardians of our children's spiritual health, because, *and very importantly*, if it is not kept intact, their sole may have difficulty healing when it is unavoidably and most assuredly injured by this world.

Those unhealed injuries as we know only too well, often lead to future problems like drug addiction, failed marriages, or violent behavior. Even when we take all of the precautions, sometimes it is still not enough.

There are so many influences outside our control that our best efforts may fall short. And many are the times, if we honestly look at ourselves in the mirror, we know that we have not always made the best effort either. We must always remember to be diligent and set the right example. As the philosopher and author of such books as "Everything I Really Need to Know, I Learned in Kindergarten", Robert Fulghum is credited with saying, *"Don't worry that children never listen to you, worry that they are always watching you."* To our children it is particularly true that *"actions speak louder than words."*

All through our years, we trip and stumble along the paths of life. When we're little we most often fall down with visible cuts and bruises.

As we age, we fall mentally and spiritually, with hidden injuries to our heart and mind.

Although we can more easily catch our children when they are small and close at hand, we need to prepare for the time when they need to catch themselves and stand without us.

Leaving our children unprepared is one of the worst sins we can make as parents. Yet, if and when events go wrong in their lives, however severe, we must be careful not to blame ourselves or others as many parents will immediately do. *"Preparation"* is the key word here.

Even Jesus as he anticipated his death on the cross, wanted to prepare his adult "children", his disciples. In the book of John, knowing that He would soon depart the physical world, Jesus needed to make sure the disciples would understand how to continue on with a relationship to God, even in his absence. That day will come for us through our relationship to our children, and we need to prepare them well in advance. Jesus wanted the Disciples to know they could survive the obstacles facing them in their future as quoted in John 16:33, *"But take heart, I have overcome the world."* In other words, He has won battles and temptations we all may face during our lives.

As parents or guardians, I believe God lays three basic challenges in front of us.

First, we must love our children unconditionally as God loves each of us. Even in the worst of situations that love should still be there. We must love them for who they are, not what they have done. We must love them only as a parent can love a child; without expectations and with total innocence. And finally, we must love them even if they do not love us.

The words of Jesus speak to us as parents in Matthew 7:9-11, *"Which of you, if his son asks for bread, will give him a stone: Or if he asks for a fish, will give him a snake? If you, then, though you are evil, know how to give good gifts to your children, how much more will your Father in heaven give good gifts to those who ask him!"* And as we know, love is the greatest gift of all.

Second, we must give them the right space in which to grow. Deuteronomy is the last of the first five books of the Old Testament. Correctly translated from Hebrew it means *"These are the words"*. As you read through its pages, it becomes evident that much of the book could be described as "these are the words *to live by and which must be instilled in your children"*. Again and again we are encouraged through the inspired passages to pass along God's word and history to our offspring. In Chapter 4 the writer is very clear about making sure God's laws, as given to Moses as the Ten Commandments, be taught to the children. *"Assemble the people before me to hear my words so that they may learn to revere me as long as they live in the land and may teach them to their children."*

I particularly like the way in Deuteronomy 6:4 after the writer has repeated, *"Love the Lord your God with all your heart and with all your soul and with all your strength,"* he goes on to say, *"Impress them on your children. Talk about them when you sit at home and when you walk along the road, when you lie down and when you get up."* I cannot imagine a better way of discussing and reinforcing the faith of our children as described by those verses. How many times have you or I passed an opportunity to talk about faith to our children.

However, like the fish constrained to a small tank, we cannot expect our children to ever grow or expand their intellect, spiritual self-awareness, or freedom of theological choice if we don't give them the space they need. And like fish seeing a glass wall every way they turn, we can't make our children bump into "God" continuously, otherwise if they do find some room to escape they might never look back for fear of being trapped again.

Ideally, we want our children to grow into godliness, not be pushed into it.

Third, God challenges us to let our children have their own life, however long or short it may be. Breaking the ties between parenting and being a parent begins when the umbilical cord is first severed and should continue until we have let our children become the master of their own world, equals among the human race, and independent in their own thoughts.

Obviously as Christians we believe that God let his son Jesus make the choice to die on the cross for us. How many of us as parents could have done that?

We need to be there for our children, not as crutches, but as coaches and cheerleaders.

As long as they know we are there for them, they will turn to us for help. Although I look at Jesus as being very independent and strong, think how many times He turned to God for assistance. Asking God for help was not a sign of weakness, but instead, a testament to His strong faith that God was there for Him, with Him, and working through Him. I want my children to feel the same about their mother and me. Don't you want the same for each child that you have or ones that may depend on you?

I can remember as if it were yesterday, helping to teach both of my boys to swim. Like many of you, I stood in the pool, coaxing them to jump into the water, holding my outstretched arms to catch them, and assuring them they would be alright. Think of the confidence they put in me when they literally took that leap of faith. No loving parent would have let their child jump and then failed to hold them above the water.

Tragically, I know a person who after losing his pre-teen daughter to cancer, has spent most of his life trying to protect his other children from the normal experiences and consequences of living. He smothered them with attention, and provided for their every need however simple or extravagant. To my knowledge, they have never been able to fully stand on their own, always relying on their father, not as a parent but mostly as a banker. I have no doubt that he loves his children, but he failed to give them an independent life, and today they live with that anchor that may forever hold them back. Like butterflies perpetually stuck as a chrysalis, they have never metamorphed into their final form - to spread their wings and fly on their own.

As I said earlier, life is a phenomenon and an event we often take for granted. It can disappear in an instant.

Sometimes reading about it in the paper or hearing about it from someone over the telephone, can make the loss of life seem distant and surreal. But to the parents, relatives and friends of the child or young adult, the pain is no fantasy. Our family has seen *four* children that for a brief period walked the same paths of our two boys and died far too early. (Sadly when I first drafted this chapter the number above was only three).

My youngest son had a friend who was killed before the age of 10, when, while standing on a curb with his father following an Atlanta Braves baseball game, he quite innocently reached over to pick up a player's bubble gum card he had dropped and was struck by a passing car. A teenage girl and classmate of my oldest son, died about a year after asking him to a sophomore dance when her car slid through a stop sign and hit a tree one rainy night. Another one of his classmates and member of his baseball team died by gunfire when the boy tried to breakup a dispute between two other teenagers in a fast-food parking lot. Finally, while writing this book, another boy, a classmate of my youngest and also the brother of a young lady that my oldest once dated died when the car his mother was driving hydroplaned into the path of an oncoming bus taking, not only her son's life but that of one of his close friends.

Were these children prepared for death? Did they believe in God? Was there security in knowing their spirit would live for eternity?

~

After we had our two boys, we decided to expand our little three bedroom, one bath, house. It had been fine when there were only the two of us, but as the boys grew, we constantly were bumping into each other's space. I drew the plans for a second story addition, and much to my surprise, it passed the city's architectural guidelines, and also got approval of the historical oversight committee, (amazing, since I had only taken one course in drafting at Georgia Tech).

Ty, my youngest, was about two and a half years old when the construction was almost complete. The contractor had built steps up to the second story, and as usual, after work I ventured up to see what had been accomplished that day. Ty had climbed the steps after me.

For what seems like only two or three seconds, I looked away from where he was standing, and in a blink of an eye he was gone. All I saw was a piece of plywood falling back into place over a hole at the top of the temporary steps.

Ty had walked out onto what he thought was solid flooring, and like a trap door, with just the weight of his little body, the planking had flipped up and dropped him fourteen feet to the wooden floor below.

For one brief moment I imagined him severely injured or dead, but as I rushed to the steps, (and only in this circumstance), was happy to hear his screams, and see him in the arms of my wife below. Although with an egg-sized bump on his head, he had managed to survive with no other injuries. With just a little change in variables, the outcome could have been entirely different . . . a broken back, a coma, or possibly death.

Children are both resilient and fragile at the same time and . . . that time, resiliency won. God was watching over us that day, but when events like that happen, it is sometimes good to remember the momentary mental pain and fear, and think about the potential consequences of what could have happened and be thankful for what did.

Be appreciative of your children, for who they are and not for what you think they should be.

Believe it or not, in their own way, they can become butterflies and sail away as they should some day. Just remember to give them your love, the space they need, and a life of their own.

All too quickly our children will leave to discover their own destiny. Some will strike out to college, while others like my youngest son Ty, temporarily postpone higher education and set their sights on other adventures. In his case a five year stint in the Navy. Thousands will become coal miners, bricklayers, cooks, or firefighters, or fill one of the millions of jobs necessary to making our civilization civilized. And, unfortunately, some will fall into ditches of despair, waste their lives in crime, or die a premature death.

~

When the boys were about the age of a first-grader, I used to read to them a book by Shel Silverstein called "The Giving Tree". It is a remarkable five minute tale of love that chronicles the growth of a boy to manhood and then to old age all the while being supported by the tree under which he first played. No matter what the boy takes from the tree it is always there to provide what it can, even as a stump for the boy to rest on as an old man. I want my children and their children in turn to know I will always be that tree for them.

C. Everett Koop, a pediatric surgeon by training, and the Surgeon General for the United States under President Reagan is quoted as saying, *"Life affords no greater responsibility, no greater privilege, than the raising of the next generation."* Jesus made his disciples very cognizant of that fact urging them to be teachers, to establish a continuing thread of faith to God from one generation to the next. Of course it is a theme repeated not only in the New Testament of the Bible, but from the beginning of the scriptures.

Proverbs 1:8-16 is a great example. From a parent's point of view to a son (or daughter), it warns of being enticed away from Godliness and into sin; *"Listen, my son, to your father's instruction and do not forsake your mother's teaching,"* it begins. To paraphrase, *"pay attention to us, your parents, and do not ignore what we are about to tell you."* This beginning certainly sets the stage for what is to come. It gets the children's attention and positions them for the rest of what the parents want their children to hear. In this instance the verses basically warn them not to be tempted to go with the wrong crowd, *". . . do not set foot on their paths; for their feet rush into sin."* PR 1:15.

I'm reminded of a coach I once had that always started important statements with a loud *"LISTEN UP!"* And, believe me, you had better pay attention to the words that followed. Usually they were very important instructions about how the game was to be played, things to watch out for, and a plan to win. Isn't it the same with life? Isn't it what you want to tell your children?

~

Your challenge is to constantly remind children of God's presence in the universe. Even if they don't respond the way you think they should, the human mind is a marvel of creation and each child is recording everything you do and say. Their poker face may hide the processing of that information, but assuredly, it's happening. Don't ever give up - you will survive their growing up and some day they will appreciate what you have done for them (and for putting up with them).

God, on the other hand, like an all knowing parent, is always there for us. Whatever form He takes, I imagine God is everywhere. Whether you believe our universe was started with one big bang or even if you think it is but one of an infinite number of universes, God is there somewhere, waiting and guiding all that you see and don't see. Even Stephen Hawkin, who is today regarded as possibly the most intelligent scientific theorist since Albert Einstein, implies that God is the only explanation for the existence of the universe, regardless of how it was formed. We then are God's children. We live in the space and time He created.

~

Make sure you savor every moment when your children are young because events are happening at light speed! Expose them to the beauty in the universe. Give them your time and faith in God. Watch your children and observe them with love. Record their voices, take their pictures, and pack away their schoolwork and little toys because . . . all of that will be over before you realize it.

A song by country music singer Billy Dean called, *"Let Them Be Little"*, will make any parent think about the importance of their children, how quickly they grow up, and their value to our lives. If you have a chance, listen to his words as he paints a picture most of us as a mom or dad has seen and, for me, wish I could experience again rather than create only the image from just a memory.

There will be one last time you throw them in the air, one last time you hold them on your hip, one last time you change a dirty diaper, or one last time you see them cross home plate, but you will never know when that time will be . . . you'll only know that it has already happened.

Study Guide Chapter 13
Metamorphosis

Children can many times try your patience. On those occasions it seems the easier course of action is to give in, give
up, or run away from the situation. Of course, all you have
done is to move the challenge to a later time. Eventually,
if you truly love and care for your child, you will confront
the situation, develop a solution, and then put that event
behind you. Most importantly, your ultimate challenge is
to lead then down the path of Godliness through your
faith.

As you read and respond to each of the points below, keep
in mind what God would want you do to.

*1. From a child's perspective, what do you think is the
most difficult issue in transitioning (morphing) from an
adolescent to a teenager? How could you as a parent or
guardian help them with this?*

*2. Do you feel at ease talking with your children (or as an
advisor to someone else's child) about their problems?
Make a list explaining either side of your answer and then
discuss them with your spouse or a friend who has children. Afterwards, make a list of anything you learned that
throws a positive light on how, in the future, you will talk
with children.*

*3. Why does the Bible constantly refer to God as a father
figure? Is this a significant point, and if so, why?*

*4. If you have older children, what points of wisdom would
you have liked to have told them when they were younger?
Why?*

Group Discussion

1. Ask each member to pick the one issue they think is most difficult for a child to face today and then discuss each one. Are there trends among the group, and if so, why?

2. Discuss when is the best time to introduce God into a child's life. How would they do it if it was their responsibility?

3. What is the best way to introduce God and faith to a teenager? How is it different from a little child or an adult?

4. Is it ever OK to relinquish the teaching of societal moray's for our children to other entities such as the government or a religious institution?

5. Discuss why it is never too late to teach someone about God, regardless of their age.

Chapter XIV

BALANCING ACT

Some time ago, as a graduate student at Columbia University, Mane Christine de Lacoste[18] wrote a paper on differences in the size of certain regions of the brain. More specifically, she measured an area called the corpus collasum, a band of fibers that connect the left and right hemispheres of the brain; much the way a highway connects two cities. It is responsible for relaying most of the information between the two cerebral halves.

Among other discoveries, her research indicated a greater amount of connective bands for female subjects than males. In other words, there was the implication that more communication between the two hemispheres occurred for women than for men. This new information directly supported previous research in the thinking patterns and abilities of the two genders.

It had been assumed for a number of years prior to her research that the brains of men and women were "wired" differently. For instance, numerous tests have shown that men typically are better at math and have visually enhanced cognitive skills (like map orientation), while women are better with verbal tasks like languages.

De Lacoste's work supports a previous theory spawned by Roger Sperry, another researcher, which hypothesized men's brains were more "lateralized" in processing information. Simply stated, men typically use one half of the brain more discretely in making decisions than women. This may make it easier for men to reach an unemotional conclusion to a problem because the two parts of the brain don't work as closely together prior to certain decisions. It also means that the male, if right-handed, tends to take a more focused advantage of the right hemisphere of the brain, which controls spatially oriented functions and large motor skills. Knowing this difference first hand, I might be inclined to say, "*A man may make a faster decision, initially driving down the wrong road whereas a woman may be late to the meeting while deciding which road to take*".

Another example of this is with the advent of cable and satellite TV systems, we are sometimes offered over 100 channels from which to select. Men will tend to jump from channel to channel, virtually "hunting" for some unknown program, often settling on one channel for a few minutes (or seconds), and then moving on to another. Women, in contrast, usually take a more methodical approach, often looking at the guide before selecting a channel, and then honing in on their choice for lengthier periods before deciding to change, if ever.

None of this is to say that there is not a substantial amount of redundancy and overlap between the two genders, nor does it imply that given the same information, the two sexes cannot reach the same conclusion. The male may put more mileage on the car, drive faster, and arrive at the meeting without the use of a map, while the female might take a shorter path though somewhat slower, more methodical and cautious in her transit.

In primitive societies, this may account for men being able to easily find their way back from long hunting sojourns, while the women are better equipped mentally to nurture the young, tasks requiring more emotional or communicative skills.

The pairing of the male and female, aside from procreation, is God's way of producing a balanced union of abilities; both physically and mentally.

It is important for us to realize this when we are married and give way to each other's innate abilities. Yet, our individualism and self-inflated egos often create a tremendous obstacle to reaching a balance with our spouse. It is one challenge of marriage that never seems to fully vanish as much as we may try.

Today in the United States, the divorce rate is a little over 1% per 100 people per year. The information reported by the Centers for Disease Control (CDC) in Atlanta was for the period from 2006-2007, (I'm not sure why the CDC would be reporting this, but to many, divorce is like a disease isn't it!). Luckily the rate has been trending down in recent years from it's high in 1981, peaking at 5.3 divorces per 1000 people to about 3.6 in 2007 as cited in a May 2007 USA Today article. Obviously it is still far to high. It shows that we are not very good in facing the challenges marriage brings to us.

People often try to evaluate when a divorce is justified, going to others to help answer the question. In Matthew 19:8, Jesus replied, *"Moses permitted you to divorce your wives because your hearts were hard. But it was not this way from the beginning. 9 I tell you that anyone who divorces his wife, except for marital unfaithfulness, and marries another woman commits adultery."* To many this seems a harsh and unforgiving statement.

However, what it does emphasize is that marriage should not be taken lightly and unless there are severe and extenuating circumstances, infidelity for example, it should be held together. Marriage should be respected and valued. Of course, if the individuals do not respect each other, how can they respect their marriage?

~

Except for biscuits and muffins, I follow the path of most men in the kitchen by experimenting, creating a big mess, and usually producing bad results that only I will eat. My wife, in contrast, can finesse a good meal out of most any ingredients, yet I would not want her in my workshop among the large power tools for fear of her losing a finger or other disastrous consequences.

I love my wife of over 35 years for not just her great cooking, but what she figuratively "brings to the table" and believe she feels the same about me. I certainly hope she appreciates more than my charm, good looks, and ability to carry large baskets of clothes upstairs for her. In addition, I recognize that if I try to take an unbalanced approach to decisions that affect the family, it most likely will result in a poorer decision if she is not involved. Could I function without her? The real question is, *"Would I want to function without her?"* And the answer is an overwhelming, *"No!"*

In Proverbs 12:6, the first part of that verse states, *"A wife of noble character is her husband's crown"*. Some Biblical scholars believe this directly reflects back to the book of Ruth, a short story about the unselfish love of a wife toward her family, and indirectly reinforces the strength of King David's ancestry. It is also an example of the importance of one spouse to fulfilling the values that God wants, and is an integral resource to any family that is faith-based. My wife has always tried to set that type of value for our family.

Ellie and I met at a little Methodist College in the mountains of north Georgia called Reinhardt (now a university). She was a freshman, and I had temporarily transferred from Georgia Tech as a second quarter sophomore in order to salvage my grades, (which were within a fraction of having me booted out). Unfortunately too much attention to fraternities, weekly parties, and dates at least twice a week, was not the formula for success at a school that demanded much more than a wee bit of studying.

Although I had been dating someone at Agnes Scott College, it soon became clear that the 60 mile separation was causing our relationship to deteriorate. (Additionally, I'm not sure her dad who was a high-ranking officer in the Army thought much of the often out-spoken and somewhat naive 19 year-old she was seeing, so having me far removed from his daughter was probably just fine with him). After a few weeks, I began to realize the relationship was coming to a rapid end and decided to commence dating at Reinhardt.

Ellie was one of the first girls I had met, but because my understanding was that she was involved with someone else, I dated several other young women including her roommate during that quarter, but continued to reflect on the possibility of asking her out. A few months later in March, as if by a divine plan, my intended date to a cookout (hay ride and all), discovered a conflict the day of the event and could not go.

Spotting Ellie on the tennis courts a little while later that morning, I struck up a conversation, walked with her back to the dorm, determined that she did not have a date that evening, and as she bounced the ball against the floor, asked her to go. Without more that a second's hesitation, she said, *"No"*. I stood there dumbfounded, not expecting such a fast rejection with no explanation, but while my jaw was still dropped, she said, *"What did you just ask me?"* I repeated the invitation and this time she said, *"Yes"*.

That one conversation, that first "Yes", was the beginning of what has been many wonderful and sometimes challenging years together. It has meant that as my partner she should always be part of my mind and spirit, even when we do not agree.

There are thousands of "yes and no's", and "right or left's" that we encounter in life that influence where we go - what paths we take. And, any one of them can be a deciding factor in determining how our life will ultimately be measured. For me, I cannot think of a better pivoting point in my life than when she said "yes" those many years ago.

Ellie adds the thoughtfulness that I often lack when verbalizing my ideas or comments. She represents the deeper caring for emotional values that I so easily overlook. She teaches me to approach life by reining in some of my tendencies to move full steam ahead regardless of incoming torpedoes. And, most important during our early years of marriage, she maintained her faith during a period of time when I tried to ignore my own.

As husbands or wives, we need to appreciate both the similarities and differences in the other spouse. God challenges each of us to overlook the imperfections we all have and accept our partner for their positive assets.

Their value should not be measured in material productivity, numbers of clubs or social events in which they participate, or a title they have achieved. When people talk about "surviving a marriage", I want them to think about it in terms as two partners, surviving life's challenges together, as a team.

Many years ago, Bill Cosby, an American comic, actor, and someone known to express his philosophy on life, wrote a book called, "Love and Marriage". I would do it injustice to try and pull just one sentence from it without placing it in context. However, for anyone contemplating marriage or already married, it is a wonderful description of a person's voyage into the realm and reality of living as a couple and how to keep it intact. It reminds me of the little things that go into making such a partnership work.

~

The seventh chapter of Corinthians is entirely concerned with Paul's feelings about the sanctity and responsibility of both partners in marriage. It is clear that he sees them as equals when he states in verse 4, *"The wife's body does not belong to her alone but also to her husband. In the same way, the husband's body does not belong to him alone but also to his wife."* Although some interpret this as only referring to sexual relations, in contrast, many believe that the word "body" also means the entire being, both physical and emotional; both the mind and the spirit. Yet, the writer Paul also talks about each as an individual in partnership with the other as well, defining their duties, even as a spouse of a non-believer in Christ.

As anyone who has ever played on a team knows, there are times when each participant functions with almost anonymity so that the whole becomes greater than its parts.

When disciplining children, I have learned too many times, that parenting is most effective when the husband and wife function as a unified team.

Children, like in jungle warfare, can easily create strategies to pick off their targets and win their skirmishes with parents, if the "army" is divided. (Remember the old phrase, "divide and conquer"? Believe me, it's true!) Kids can make things so confused, that the parents end up fighting, much like soldiers shooting at each other when lost in the dark.

Yet, there is also the importance of the individual player. Each spouse must know they are truly respected by the other. They must be given the ability to grow and express their talents in meaningful ways, without negative criticism, and with the encouragement only a loving spouse can give. God challenges us to be receptive of the change our spouse can bring, *even at those times we are not asking for a change.* We must place ourselves in our partner's shoes, learning to view the world through their eyes. However, it does not mean we must sit passively while they move forward with what we may think is a bad decision.

There are too many instances where a career has dictated that the family move to another location and, without adequate participation in the decision by both spouses, the change has ended in a disaster. How many times has a sports enthusiast been *marketed* into buying the largest television system available without ever consulting with their marriage partner to see if the money could have satisfied something for which they both could have benefitted? Maybe the answer would be, *"Sure honey, get the TV . . . we will both enjoy watching movies together on the bigger screen."* (I haven't heard that from my wife yet, so the five year old 30 inch set is still in the den.)

Obviously, the best decision is a mutual decision.

It may not always be possibly, but if that is the intended goal, then there is a much better chance it will be achieved.

John Steinbeck, the American author once said, *"A journey is like marriage. The certain way to go wrong is to think you can control it"*. No one spouse should have more authority or control than the other unless one becomes physically or mentally handicapped. Even then, there are limitations. Yet, how often will a husband or wife treat the other as if they have already become incapacitated?

I have always been amazed that some societies of the world place greater worth in one of the marriage partners over the other . . . usually the male. Even certain religions perpetuate that idea.

The problem many of us have is trying to use the wrong scale to measure each others value.

How often has one spouse used the phrase, *"I make most of the money, so I should determine how it is spent"*. WRONG! It may seem like the right defensive position to take when you've just spent money you should not have and guilt is sitting on your shoulder, but believe me it never works! What if the other marriage partner had not been home to keep the kids from burning the house down? What if the other spouse was a teacher, inspiring people to make more of their lives? Or, what if your spouse had loved you so much as to put their aspirations aside so you could pursue yours?

So, what kind of scale do we use?

The scale must never measure the value of marriage partners quantitatively.

In other words, not in dollars, weight, achievements, or looks . . . nothing that you can tangibly see or touch should be used as a form of measurement. Instead, *we must always perceive the scale as balanced by what we see in our mind, and feel in our heart.*

If we believe in God, then we should also believe He challenges each of us to see through the physical world and find the intangible attributes of value. This is true not only for how we should perceive everyone, but particularly for our spouse. It is a very difficult challenge when you consider all the messages we are constantly bombarded with that seem to emphasize only the physical aspects of our lives; the big houses, beautiful cars, athletic bodies, and expensive vacations. Sadly, although these are of the least importance on the scale of human values, they are most often unrecognized for what they are.

As we grow older, I believe we begin to appreciate each other more fully. Maybe it's because we mature in our thinking, have continued to accept our differences, and realize we both are trying to do the best we can, although continuing to be fallible like all humans.

In all likelihood, Ellie or I will die before the other. I rarely think about that occurrence, inevitable as it is. But when that time comes, I believe whoever outlives the other will be left with a wonderful collection of memories about our lives together, the obstacles we overcame, the children we raised, and the fun we had. We should remember the little things like recovering some abandoned kittens from the side of the road, spending a summer painting the outside of our house, Ellie learning to shift gears in my 1963 Austin Healey sports car, or walking around at Christmas time with a drop cord light hooked to the only receptacle with electricity when our old house was being remodeled.

We are reminded throughout the Bible that our spirit will continue to exist long after our body has turned back into its structural elements at death. Only through faith in God can we also believe we will forever be united with our life's partner after we die.

What will you remember about your partner? How will you have measured on the only scale that matters?

Remember, it's never too late to put your life and relationships in balance.

Study Guide Chapter 14
Balancing Act

In today's world as it was thousands of years ago, conflict between two partners in marriage can lead to relational instability, misery, and, all too often, divorce. Yet, are we failing to consider the basics of the relationship, how it was conceived and upon what foundation was it built? God gives us direction throughout the Bible if only we pay attention. However, we have to be careful to understand how that advice was given and in what context.

Different societies and religions have often imbued unequal value to one marriage partner over the other. Even in the Christian faith, beliefs differ widely. As you or your group review each of the discussion points and questions below, keep those differences in perspective.

1. Do you see the relationship between a man and woman as equal, and if so, why? Write down each reason and then try and value each against the other. In other words, for each asset one gender has, is there a balanced asset the other brings to a relationship? If equal in your eyes, then is there a difference in God's perspective? (Read Genesis 2:18-24)

2. If you were to list all of the attributes of your spouse (if married), how often do you fail to appreciate each one? (If you are single, what attributes do you think would be valuable in a marriage partner and why?) Write each one down along with the explanation and then discuss with someone who is married.

3. If you made a list in number "2" above, select one attribute and tell your spouse today how much you value that asset he or she has. (If you are dating or considering marriage, do the same - pick an attribute you appreciate and tell the other person.)

4. We often hear the phrase, "give and take" as it relates to the interaction of two people. What does that mean to you as it relates to a partner in marriage, and more specifically to your partner if married? Look in the Bible to see if God expects this type of relationship between a husband and a wife.

Group Discussion:

For numbers 1 and 2 below, read Ephesians 6:22-30.

1. Is the writer saying that wives must always follow the requests of their husbands? Explain each member's answer and then discuss.

2. How is the relationship of a husband and wife similar to Christ and the church? How important is love to this equation as it is described?

3. If any member of the group has gone through a divorce, (and only if they are comfortable discussing it) look at question "2" in the individual section and have them describe the attributes their spouse had when they were first married. Was a change in one or more of them responsible for the divorce or was it a change in the group member's attributes?

4. Why do arranged marriages (still prevalent in parts of the world) typically have no higher divorce rates than those that follow a more traditional courtship?

Chapter XV

STANDING TALL

After a fire has destroyed a forest, the first species of trees to begin reclaiming the denuded ground are the conifers . . . the pine, fir, spruce, cedar and other cone-bearing plants. They are the most easily spread by animals, are quickest to sprout, and grow more rapidly than the hardwood trees like oak, elm, and hickory. They also thrive on sunlight, and so the open areas provided by the scorched earth give them more than adequate opportunities to flourish. But as anyone familiar with wood knows, timber from trees like the pine or fir is softer, more brittle, subject to insect damage, and warps easily.

Being from the southern part of the United States, we have a generous amount of pines, and although they can provide wonderful greenery and shade throughout the year, they can also be a real headache when on those rare occasions we have a winter mix of ice and snow. The weight of their ice-covered needles will cause them to snap and break, often taking electrical lines with them, not to mention the mess they make in our yards and streets. There has been more than one time in my life, which I have suffered through two or more days without electricity because of their frailty.

Unfortunately, if a substantial portion of the top of a conifer is broken out, it will not survive. This is particularly true of pines. For years they stand as ugly reminders of past storms, rapidly rotting, becoming infested with insects, and occasionally providing a home to a bird such as a woodpecker. Eventually they fall when decay finally takes their last bit of strength.

If a forest is left unmanaged by mankind, eventually the conifers will give way to the slower-growing hardwoods. Although it may take as long as fifty or more years, once the hardwood trees are able to tower above the pines, firs, etc., their canopy of leaves will begin to slow the growth of the conifers, eventually causing them to die.

There is nothing more majestic than a mature hardwood forest, yet sadly, in most of the developed nations of the earth, there are few of these forests remaining. The grandeur of seeing a poplar tree that is over 350 years old is truly a God-inspiring sight! Of course these trees are just "babies" when compared to the bristlecone pines found in six western U.S. states, some measuring over 4500 years old. Their image readily shows the suffering and challenges they have endured to stay alive over all of the millennia.[19]

We are like the trees in the forest.

When we are young, if given a reasonable environment, we grow rapidly, seeking the "light" from those around us. Our parents, if they love us, will make sure we get adequate nourishment, both physical and spiritual. Yet, it is eventually up to us to determine if we will become an oak or pine; to have internal strength that will carry us through the storms of life, or allow us to become broken down, easily attacked by our environment, or decay from inside. In other words, however long our life, only we can decide if we will have the fiber of a hardwood like an oak, or the softness of a pine.

None of us when we are born have any idea how long our life will be. As we age though, we can begin to sense what purpose our life has and to some extent help determine our final destiny.

It seems clear that many of the biblical prophets realized what the future held for them and so too did Jesus. Soon after he was baptized, he began to preach the word of God, focused on his mission on Earth, and knowing he would be sacrificed to save others.

In Matthew 20:18 Jesus told the Disciples of his pending fate and referring to himself in the third person stated, *"They will condemn him to death and will turn him over to the Gentiles to be mocked and flogged and crucified."* Yet, even knowing how and when He would die, He never stopped giving of himself to others. Jesus saw meaning in every day he had on this planet.

Becoming older is not something to fear, but to look forward to. I remember when I was about seven years old a friend and I were playing with little army figures (the kind where a two-dollar bag would give you an entire regiment - you picked the color). A group of real "old" kids, probably thirteen or fourteen, came by and watched us for a while. I remember asking one of them what grade they were in, and one of them answered, *"high school"*.

I still remember saying to them, *"I wish I were in high school."*

One of them replied, *"No you don't. I wish I were your age again."* Another of the boys standing there reaffirmed the comment.

I was really surprised when they said what they did! *"Who in their right mind"*, I thought, *"would want to be little like us when, if you were big, there would be so much more you could do?"*

Isn't it funny, that when we are young, we can't seem to wait until we are older . . . and when we are older, we wish we were young again?

If asked, many of us are quick to state all of the goals and accomplishments we want in life, yet as we move further along in years, we often find ourselves not meeting those expectations. In a way, it's like those New Year's resolutions we make. As lofty or insignificant as they may be, few are the ones we actually accomplish. Maybe that's why we would like to go back in time, to start over again, to have another chance to do it right. Otherwise, if we were satisfied with what we have done and happy with where life is taking us, why would we want to turn the clock back? On the other hand, maybe we are putting the emphasis on the wrong goals altogether.

Rick Warren's book "The Purpose Driven Life", is devoted to making us think about and guide us in determining our true reason for being placed on this earth. His first sentence of the first chapter sets the premise, *"It's not about you."*

So much of what most of us do as we become older is to set our goals on things that only benefit ourselves.

And when we reach the end of our lives what value have we created because of those series of big and little choices that were self-centered?

Our society continuously places chronological markers in our life . . . how old we have to be to start school, the proper age to get a driver's license, the point in time that you legally become an adult.

At a simpler level, in one African tribe, manhood is reached when a boy survives the kill of his first wild pig. Then there are the actuaries that tell us what our expected age will be before we die, how many of us will have heart attacks or cancer, or be hit by lightning. If it were not for some "committee" setting these arbitrary dates, would any of it really matter as many seem to believe?

> *We appear to be so programmed to move forward to the next marker that we may be failing to take advantage of where we are at any one moment in life.*

Look at how many child movie stars have had disastrous lives as adults. Was it because they never had the chance to have a child's life?

Being fixated on either moving forward or wanting to go back may waste so much of our effort that when we reach the twilight of our life we have less to show for it than if we had been more judicious with our time.

Where are the truly important markers in life and who is telling us what they are? Aren't there some pretty good indications in the Bible?

Wouldn't you much rather be remembered for the number of smiles you brought to a child, the number of people you befriended, or the skills you passed as a mentor? It seems to me these are the markers that epitomize the wishes of God and becomes the legacy we can create as we age.

Matthew 7:17-20 "*. . . every good tree bears good fruit, but a bad tree bears bad fruit. A good tree cannot bear bad fruit, and a bad tree cannot bear good fruit. Every tree that does not bear good fruit is cut down and thrown into the fire. Thus, by their fruit you will recognize them.*"

With the exception of her thirtieth, my wife Ellie has always seemed to take each birthday in stride. On that particular date she actually cried. In her mind, no longer being in her twenties seemed to be a significant change, although to me she was just as pretty as she had been the day before (and still is). Twenty-four hours later she seemed to be over the event, continuing along the path of being a great mom and wife, and wasn't that the important part of being on earth another day rather than not being twenty nine instead of thirty?

I'm as fallible as anyone to succumbing to the temptation to reverse time. It seems like everyday when I look in the mirror to shave, there's another wrinkle, gray hair, or some part of my body that is moving out of position . . . time to hit the treadmill, cut back on the carbohydrates, apply some more skin toner. No matter how I might want it to change, so far, aging remains an inevitable process, so I'd better make the most of the time I have!

More recently I decided there is a way to tell when you're really getting old. It's when you can't find a radio station playing your "oldies" anymore. Based on a trip in my car to Tennessee recently, I discovered I must be at that point in life after scanning the airwaves for most of an hour.

Accepting the fact that we are getting older is a difficult challenge God places in front of everyone. In one way it is to admit that each passing year brings us closer to death. To me that is the worst way of thinking about aging.

On the other hand, some people try and ignore the fact entirely, while still others spend enormous amounts of money cosmetically altering their bodies to appear younger. (Maybe looking better does make you feel happier or boost your confidence, and so I would certainly never say it is wrong.) Instead though, why not believe that the challenge of getting older is to see how productive you can be with your time on Earth, however long or short.

Jesus died a young man in his thirties yet look at what he accomplished in such a very short time . . . mostly compressed into a span of about three years.

The majority of you reading this have at least three years to do something, do you not? And even if you have but one day, is there not something you can do to help someone else, offer hope, show compassion, lend a listening ear?

---

*The mirror of your life is the truest reflection
of who you are.*

Although it may not be quickly apparent, if you look around carefully, you will see it, touch it, and feel it. Peer into the faces of those you love, hear the concern you bring to people, and feel the hugs back from those being hugged. Are you spending time polishing the mirror or are there cracks and smudges that distort what you want it to be?

---

*Growing older should be a truly remarkable experi-
ence . . . an experience worth making remarks about!*

It should also stand as a foundation for our actions. As Will Rogers once said, *"Good judgment comes from experience, and a lot of that comes from bad judgment."*

Trying your hand at having a productive life does not mean it will not have negative consequences. Nor will it be clear of what may seem like insurmountable hills to climb. In other words, like all humans you'll make mistakes, but faith with help you learn by them. And although we may be aging every second of every day, God never ages! His message is as fresh today as it was in the beginning and as it will be for all eternity. He is there always to help with every challenge he puts before us.

Like many, if it were not for my faith I would find myself as a pine tree, quickly growing up but with little internal strength, too easily broken by a passing storm, and never standing tall and strong as a hardwood.

*I want to be a shade maker and not wither
in someone else's shadow.*

And when I fall for the last time I want it to be with a loud crash from the weight of what I have accomplished rather than a muffled sound of decaying timber.

~

Someone wrote in my high school yearbook, *"Remember the mighty oak grew from a nut like you!"* It was one of those silly remarks that kids often write, but in reality, I would rather be the mighty oak. The seed is in each of us and we have the gift of God to determine the species of tree into which it will grow.

For those who know me well, they also know I am the consummate "pack rat". I hate to throw anything away. But there are a lot of little things special to me I keep that if all else were lost, they would still encapsulate much of what I have done over the years. I have a box that contains bits and pieces of my life - reminders of my past experiences so that some day, if my gray matter is not working quite as well as it is now, I can use them to open those memories tucked away in my mind.

There is a Boy Scout whistle on a lanyard I made at camp one summer; one of many summers of camping and counseling with friends. There is a coin wrapped in a piece of notebook paper with a scribbled note about giving it to my children in the future (I wrote this when I was about ten). An old *Case* brand knife that my grandfather used is in the box and reminds me of the time he spent with me as a child, telling stories, going fishing, and carving the wooden pegs that held the fence gate shut. I also have cards from my wife, my parents, and my children telling me how wonderful I am (maybe some of it was true). There are probably a hundred such pieces in all. Everyone should have a box like this to remind him or her how great life is and how much we should appreciate each and every bit of it.

I hope God gives me many more years to add to this box, but if I were to die tomorrow, at least I know I have worked to grow older with greater understanding, positive accomplishments, and fewer regrets. But like any person, if given the chance, I would certainly go back in time and do some things differently (and hopefully, better).

After thirteen years in a wonderful neighborhood in a small community called Vinings, Ellie and I decided it was time to downsize. We were about to become empty nesters with our youngest son scheduled to go into the Navy at the end of summer. We desperately needed to eliminate some extra space we would no longer require.

Our oldest son dropped by to pack his room (vacated six years earlier) a few days before the move. Our youngest son finished packing his room just minutes ahead of the movers. It was interesting to see what they selected to keep as they sorted through all of their possessions.(It was also very interesting to see what they threw away as we went about emptying their trash cans - some of which we quickly elected to retrieve!)

Like most, they had kept the trophies of their youth, favorite photos of friends, books they had enjoyed, and stacks and stacks of baseball cards. Yet for me,(and very selfishly I must admit), I was happy to see them keep things that only had value because I had given those items to them. In a way it was a part of me they had made a conscious decision to keep. Some day when I am no longer alive, I hope those things will remind Eric and Ty of my love for each of them rather than stir memories of times we may have argued over some insignificant issue that seemed all too significant when it occurred.

Erma Bombeck, a very funny lady and a joy to listen to, who, as she was dying from cancer, wrote very seriously about her regrets in life. Among the many things she listed in a work titled, "If I Had My Life To Live Over", was: *"I would have sat on the lawn with my children and not worried about grass stains."*

So many of us live with those same kind of regrets and yet, unlike Erma who died in 1996, we still have a chance to change the situation. And although she positively influenced many people to enjoy their lives, their children, and their families through humorous reflection, she also realized there was more she could have done . . . more she would have changed. And thankfully, she took the time to pass those thoughts (and recommendations) on to us. Obviously, we certainly don't have to wait until we are dying to make a difference.

On another occasion she also said, *"When I stand before God at the end of my life, I would hope that I would not have a single bit of talent left, and could say, I used everything you gave me."*

I believe God wants us to live each day to it's fullest; to relish in its joys, survive through its hardships, and to remember all the positive aspects this world has to offer.

---

*Part of living each day is to live part
of it with God.*

Even if we live to be a hundred, with backs bent from age, or twisted fingers from disease, we can still stand tall as any tree in the great hardwood forests . . . knowing we have grown old with dignity because we have respected those our lives have touched, been guided by the hand of God, and successfully survived His challenges.

Study Guide Chapter 15
Standing Tall

This final chapter of the book is hinged on the importance each of us can make as an individual contributor. Furthermore, it focuses on how we need to live our lives to the fullest. The last thing we need to do is to spend most of our time worrying about the future. Obviously the future is important, but so is the present.

In light of how we can make the most of what we have and at the same time have the spiritual strength to live righteously, consider the following.

1. If given all the riches you would ever desire, what types of action would you take to remain humble?

2. Can you think of an example where Jesus told someone else how they could be a positive influence to those around them? If so, what motivated Him to say what he did to this person?

3. Have you ever contemplated what you could do with the remainder of your life that could stand apart from others in a positive way? Make a list and consider how many you could possibly accomplish.

4. Are there goals you have not achieved? How important are they? Should their priorities be changed, and if so, why?

Group Discussion

Over the past several months, two individuals I have known for many years have made the decision to become priests. Both were over the age of 50 when they were

187

inspired to do this. At first I was surprised but later realized they were electing to strengthen their stance in the
forest around them. They wanted to be shade makers in
ways they had never been before.

*1. Discuss why a business person might want to change not
only careers, but move into a totally different venue related
to religion.*

*2. How difficult is it to stand tall in a world that often
presses for uniformity or makes negative comments if you
try to take a morally higher road to success? Have each
member discuss instances where they have been faced with
that type of situation.*

*3. If an individual is physically or mentally impaired, how
can they potentially stand tall in the world that often treats
them without compassion or understanding?*

*4. Does God grant all people the opportunity to be tall in
the forest of mankind? Why does it appear there is inequal-
ity?*

*5. Have each person comment on the following . . . "some
day when you die, what would you like to be written on
your grave marker?"*

FINAL COMMENTS

As Pat Conroy, a noted Southern author once told me many, many, years ago, *"One of the hardest things about writing a book is finishing it."* Maybe this is something that all published authors say to those going in that direction, but he was absolutely right. Every time I thought the book was finished, someone would tell me to add just a bit more. (That's how the study guides were developed). And then there was my own inclination to rewrite sections for clarity or to put in one more analogy.

Well, I've concluded this version, yet I know there are many more stories about overcoming challenges God puts before us. So, in anticipation of writing another book, I would like to hear from readers that know of personal situations they or someone close to them have faced where challenges were met and overcome. Please send them to:

Surviving@SurvivingGod.org

I also welcome your comments. At the current time, you can email them to:

kig@SurvivingGod.org

or find me through "Facebook" or "LinkedIn".

Notes and Research:

1. DNA - tracing Hawaiian heritage through cellular testing and other theories: http://polynesianlineage.tripod.com/polynesians/; www.royalhawaiiancatamaran.com/ fact_about_hawaii_discovery_and_settlement.html; There appears to be no definitive date as to when the islands were settled but generally thought to be over 1500 years ago.

2. How much water is required to survive over short periods is different from what a human should intake. Health officials usually recommend a much higher level than the one quart cited to sustain normal body functions - upwards of 2 or more quarts/day; www.mayoclinic.com; www.bbc.co.uk/ health/treatments/healthy_living/nutrition/healthy_water.shtml; Food intake-www.health.gov/dietaryguidelines/; Usually a human can survive without food longer than without water.

3. Life spans of elephants can be 70 or older, while the ephemera insect lives usually less than one day. Use the internet with the following search term to discover various ages of animals, "life span of (name of animal)".

4. Cantor Fitzgerald was located on the top two floors of 1 World Trade Center. Employees were trapped above the point where the passenger jet hit the building and had no way to escape.

5. www.madd.org (Mothers Against Drunk Driving)

6. Statistics on Home Depot, 1st quarter, 2010; http://corporate.homedepot.com

7. www.thekrogerco.com; www.ohiohistorycentral.com; http://en.wikipedia.org/ wki/bernard_kroger; Bernard Henry Kroger, 1860-1938

8. R.I.F is an acronym for "reduction in force". You could also consider it a euphemism since it is a substitute for, "being let go", or "mass layoffs" or "firings".

9. www.baseball-reference.com; http://mlb.fanhouse.com; www.recoveryconnection.com

10. www.nytimes.com/2009/04/21/health/21well.html; http://ajph.aphapublications.org/ cgi/repring/ajph.2007.113654v1; www.myonlinewellness.com/topic/friendshiphealth

11. www.foxnews.com/story/0,2933,515986,00.html; www.globalsecurity.org/military/systems

12. www.spaceref.com/news/viewpr.html?pid=634; www.nasa.gov; www.universetoday.com; The "Drake" equation also attempts to estimate a number of planets, ability to sustain life, etc., although there is substantial disagreement as to the accuracy or data on which it is based.

13. www.sadd.org/stats.htm; www.suicide.org; www.nimh.nih.gov

14. www.census.gov/hhes/www/poverty/

15. www.sweetonionsource.com; http://greekfood.about.com; www.onions-usa.org

16. Dr. Maya Angelou is an accomplished poet, educator, playwright, and has been active in the civil rights movement much of her life. As an African-American, she has overcome many challenges with dignity and grace. She stands as an inspiration to all of us.

17. www.peteena.com/hold.htm; www.nsf.gov; this is an ever-changing statistic for deepest hole

18. "WHY CAN'T A MAN BE MORE LIKE A WOMAN... AND VICE VERSA" Katherine Phillips

19. www.gardenguides.com; www.blueplanetbiomes.org

Your Notes/Challenges:

Your Notes/Challenges: